W9-DIM-982

WITHDRAWN

Herbert I. London

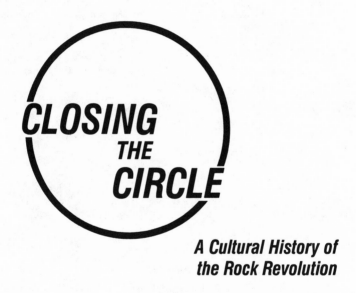

CLOSING
THE
CIRCLE

A Cultural History of
the Rock Revolution

Nelson-Hall nh Chicago

(Continued on page 198.)

LIBRARY OF CONGRESS CATALOGING IN PUBLICATION DATA

London, Herbert Ira.
  Closing the circle.

  Includes index.
  1. Rock music—History and criticism. 2. Popular culture. I. Title.
ML3534.L66   1984   784.5'4'009   84-2016
ISBN 0-8304-1057-0

CONTENTS

PROLOGUE

*T*his is a book I very much wanted to write. Having listened to rock music for thirty years, or for its entire history, and having been one of those freaks who memorized the labels and the names of groups and flip side trivia, I count rock music as part of my background the way baseball statistics are to old Brooklyn Dodgers fans. This fascination with the music took two professional forms. As a singer with a good voice who could easily imitate Presley, I impressed my friends at fraternity parties with my rendition of "Hound Dog." By the time I was nineteen, I had obviously impressed others: I had secured a record contract and was on my way to fulfilling adolescent fantasies. My second professional encounter with rock is as an academic who writes and thinks about mass culture. It has long been my opinion that rock music is a sensitive gauge of public attitudes and as such can be a useful contemporary archive for researchers were it not for their snobbish disapproval of the music.

I don't pretend to be an expert about the music, although I'm not sure what the experts know that I don't. But I have experienced this rock history as an insider and do believe there are insights I have that have not been mentioned in other books on the subject. This is not to suggest, as Goethe did, that ''only someone who has himself experienced history can make judgments about it.'' There is a lot I haven't experienced that I make judgments about, and I rely on many excellent sources who did not have historical experience, yet make superb judgments.

This, by the way, is not strictly a book on rock music. It is a cultural history with a focus on rock. It is an attempt to explore the music as a litmus test for the stages in what I will cite as a revolution in sensibilities. Many people who like rock will object to my analysis of the music as a social phenomenon. Rock, they argue, is fun; that's what it should remain. I can't argue with that, although I do believe it is more than fun. Others—perhaps the critics of the music—will argue that I have ignored record X or Y or stacked the deck to support my thesis. To these critics, I can only suggest that I made every effort to be fair, albeit my bias is sometimes apparent and occasionally blatant. I also readily admit that not every artist or group is included. Some of my favorites—like Chicago; Blood, Sweat and Tears; and the ''cross-over king,'' Ray Charles—are not mentioned.

I expect the charge that I want to downgrade or upgrade the music; that I either elevate its importance or superciliously deny its value. To these charges I can assuredly plead innocent. Rock music in this book is a tool of analysis. If one accepts my hypothesis that it mirrors cultural values, it is an excellent exploratory device for making judgments about modern life. In a sense, rarely considered by academics, rock has some scholarly value. I also want to assure the reader that I am not like the hero in Ignatius J. Reilly's *A Confederacy of Dunces,* who attends every romantic musical in his neighborhood so that he can scream at the movie screen, ''Oh my God, what degenerate produced this abortion?!'' I don't listen to rock records in order to criticize the music. Some of it is trash and some has real musical value; but those judgments tend to be far too personal for generalizations. I have long believed—like most eastern Europeans—that if you spend your whole life observing the mistakes of others, you will not live long enough to make them all yourself. I am therefore casting very few stones and doing a lot of observation.

The last point I wish to make here is that music is very much related to the politics and social life of the culture. That is as true today as it was in classical Greece or Renaissance Italy. Andrew Fletcher of Saltoun was quoted by Thomas Carlyle to have said, ''Let me make the songs of a people, and you shall make its laws.'' Music can affect people as profoundly as politics if not more so. Anyone who marched into battle amid martial music can tell you that, as can sweethearts whose romance was accompanied by their favorite song.

In writing a book of this kind there are many people to thank: My wife for her forebearance; my daughters for their understanding, especially when they required help with their homework; my secretary, who could easily be a cryptographer; my research assistant for her persistence; the many people in the industry who gave me interviews; the record company officials for their cooperation; and to Murray the K, whose support was a source of inspiration and whose death was a deep emotional blow.

Last, I should note that this book has no prescriptions; I am willing to take the heat for my theories, but I like to believe I've explained the condition of the patient. In other words, I've written this book to explain something to myself. In the process I hope that I've explained something to others.

H.I.L.

ONE

UNDER THE ROCK

*W*alking through Washington Square Park on a balmy spring day, one can't avoid the rites of the season: A waft of marijuana smoke, roller skaters moving to the rhythms of their radio earphones, volleyball players warming up by hitting a ball back and forth over an imaginary net, children by the score scurrying busily about in the sandbox, old people planting seeds in a corner of the park that hasn't been denuded by hoodlums, and the chess players who arrive with the first warm day to try a new opening move.

Coloring this pastiche is the omnipresent music—rock music. It can be heard in loud, violent bursts from radios that resemble suitcases; it is splashed on the canvas of sound by guitar players with harmonicas in their mouths, and it resounds through the air as street singers use the echo effect under the arch to parody the Flamingos, Coasters, Silhouettes, and other fifties rock groups.

The one extraordinary condition of this scene is the ubiquity of the music. Kids and adults, junkies and businessmen, dropouts and graduate students are caught in the mysterious attraction of the rock rhythm. I've often wondered why rock

1

seems to cut across so many barriers of class, age, and ethnicity. What possible meaning can it have to attract such a paradoxically heterogeneous audience? I've asked this question many times, but I never before tried to get an answer. However, in this, the summer of 1981, I searched for answers.

I stopped a roller skater floating through the streets as if transported by a spirit. Her lilting, sexy, side-to-side motion gave her the appearance of a snake in overdrive.

"Excuse me, could you please tell me what rock music means to you?"

"Means to me? Are you crazy, rock is everything. It's my fuel, my energy. If I take my plugs out I can't skate. I can't move without that music. There used to be a time when I needed milk, then bread, now all I need is music. It's my spiritual nourishment, man."

Her colorful language appeared contrived, but there was no reason to question the genuine quality of her sentiments. I went on looking for a different kind of rock aficionado, one less flamboyant, less inclined to levitation. He wasn't hard to find. When I asked this student from New York University what rock meant to him, he looked at me with a wry grin.

"Rock has no meaning, it's all mood. I don't listen to words, I hear sounds."

I wasn't surprised by this reply, but I didn't realize how prevalent a view it is. "Rock is bubblegum;" "I dig the beat;" "it crashes my mind;" "it makes me move;" "I love the sound;" "I like it hot and dirty" are comments that attest to rock's nonverbal appeal. Curiously, those few who did attribute meaning to the lyrics had selective and idiosyncratic interpretations.

As I was busy chatting and taking notes, a long haired fellow with one earring prominently displayed intruded on my conversation. He couldn't wait for my question. "Rock promotes revolution by tearing down conventions. If you 'Can't Get No Satisfaction' then you begin to see the system as bankrupt."

When I suggested that record companies represent large businesses that have a stake in the system, the park revolutionary smiled before arguing, "Lenin said the West will sell us the rope we'll use to hang them. Those records are rope; they produce awareness, they make the young ready for revolution."

I played the devil's advocate.

"The fact is that rock is thirty years old and conservative views are on the rise, Ronald Reagan is in the White House, and a Moral Majority is a cultural force of formidable proportions."

"Jus' wait, it's coming, jus' wait," he replied.

He shrugged his shoulders, winked, and walked away. Was this the rock millenarian waiting for an "inevitable" revolution that the lyrics of rock would help promote?

The Washington Square scene is exhilarating, but it is as representative of musical tastes as Nathan's hot dogs are of sausages. I needed a change of venue. I took the D train uptown to chat with a record producer, wondering all the way if a businessman's opinions of music represent a world as removed from the youthful park habitues as Washington Square is different from his midtown office.

This man was wearing a long-sleeved T-shirt with tapered stovepipe pants. The shadows under his eyes revealed years of heavy pot smoking. His speech was fired at me in machine-gun fashion. I wanted to duck when he opened his mouth.

Rock music means money. We try to gauge what our prospective audience wants to hear. Then we give it to them. Most of the time romance works. If it's too heavy, we lose an audience. The key is to have a sound that catches hold, a rhythm that is irresistible. Meaning is bullshit. Attitudes change so quickly. We're trying to keep up, not lead. We want to know what kind of sound turns on a teenager who has the money to buy records. If it's a teenager who doesn't have money or doesn't buy records, we're not interested in what he thinks. If it's an adult who does buy rock records, we are interested. In this business you've got to cultivate an audience and then give them what they want. There are no secrets and there is no meaning. Everything else is shit.

In essence he was telling me "money talks and bullshit walks." It is the kind of simple message an aging academic finds refreshing. Another middle-aged business executive in the rock business concurred. This promoter, who is trying hard to conceal his age in a business for the young, had his silk shirt open to the fourth button, his hair longish on the sides, and about six ounces of gold bouncing around his neck and wrists. He is something of a caricature, but his greeting was warm and friendly and his eyes were soft. I don't know if this guy lies to artists every day or beats his wife. To me, he seemed sincere.

Rock is sexy, and sex sells. When the music turns on our audience, then cash registers ring. We want kids who are turned on and who will spend some dough to stay turned on.

Two examples hardly make an opinion poll, but somehow I felt as if I had heard arguments suggestive of a much larger sample. I then turned to someone I had known in the rock business many years before, Murray the K. Remember him? Here is the consummate rock ringmaster who a generation ago had kids singing, banging out rhythms and tapping their feet at the Brooklyn Fox and on the WINS show "Swinging Soiree." If Alan Freed was the Lenin of rock, Murray was his Trotsky. He gave this undisciplined sound cultural form. He created a language of rock, a cultural style. He associated rock with romance, rebellion, and good times. He was a one-man public relations business working to spread the gospel of rock 'n' roll.

> Look man, rock music is magic. It can cool emotions in a riot or pump them up so that a riot occurs. It can help people march into war or right out of one. Music is never neutral; it affects people, yet it reflects what are prevailing tastes. The genius of pop music is the way it reflects trends. I've always believed there were nine-year cycles in this business. Look, pop music took off in 1936 with Benny Goodman's "swing." The music was an antidote to the blahs of the depression. Nine years later, Sinatra sang sentimental ballads that were designed to cool down the martial spirit during the war. Nine years after that (1954) Elvis Presley sang "Heartbreak Hotel" and Bill Haley "Rock around the Clock." The music was a reaction against the conformity of that decade. Nine years after that the Beatles struck like a hurricane. I think their popularity was related to J.F.K.'s assassination. Their music represented a dissatisfaction with social conventions. It was a search for something to believe in, perhaps beyond "straight" behavior. Nine years after that there was Watergate and the defeat in Vietnam, but rock went about as far as it could in lyrical rebellion, any further and there would be only noise. We have run out the string on rebellion. Now rock has nowhere to go but back into its past.

He knows the business as few do. He paid his dues and forced others to pay theirs. In some ways, he is a man trapped by the business. He is the Fifth Beatle, the man adopted by the Beatles when they first came here. No one can take that away from him. But that was seventeen years ago, and the world doesn't care so much about that any more. The time went by too quickly for Murray. Good times and high living always do. If only he could recapture those days in the sixties. But who can? We are what we've experienced. In Murray's case the experience was played on 45 r.p.m. but the world moved into 33⅓. Still, he can see seven-eighths of rock history, when the "experts" are lucky if they see half.

Greil Marcus, author of *Mystery Train* (1975), described rock as "American culture," not purely youth cult. "Elvis Presley," he argued, sang Tennessee singles that "dramatize a sense of what it is to be an American; what it means, what it's worth, what the stakes of life in America might be." Elvis took "his strength from the liberating arrogance, pride and the claim to be unique that grow out of a rich and commonplace understanding of what 'democracy' and 'equality' are all about: no man is better than I am."

Carl Belz, in *The Story of Rock* (1969), described rock music simply as "folk art"—the unconscious expression of slang, not for artistic effect, but because it is real.

Charlie Gillett called rock *The Sound of the City* (1970), the aggregate cry of street kids whose voices made new music.

For Jonathan Eisen, in *The Age of Rock* (1969), rock music was born of "a revolt against the sham of Western culture. . . . As such it was profoundly subversive."

A British analyst of rock music, Dave Harker, in *One for the Money* (1980), called it "working class culture" and applied a Marxist model of class conflict to explain rock music. On the other hand, Paul Johnson wrote in the *New Statesman* (February 28, 1964) that rock music was a capitalist ploy to co-opt the potential revolutionaries and keep them "preoccupied, comatose, indolent and beyond redemption."

Richard Goldstein, in *The Poetry of Rock* (1968), contended that rock at its best was the unbridled "searing power" of youthful vitality which provided at its core a "mystical experience."

Does rock mean whatever you want? Surely that is a cop-out, a facile explanation. There is an existential reality to the music and the lyric. There are areas in which there is agreement of purpose and goal. This reality is, however, elusive. Asking people to explain the meaning of rock is sometimes asking them what they believe in. Ultimately, any explanation relies on metaphors, not facts. For our lives and our motives are not found only in knowledge.

In John Barth's *Giles Goat Boy* or Franz Kafka's *The Castle,* the characters are affected by a dramatic performance, but none knows how. Curiously, each depends on the others to give him a meaning for his actions. Each instinctively trusts the play and the story to provide an interpretation of reality. In a sense, this is like our rock music. The beat of the music is the shared experience that allows us to participate with one another in generational bonding. A myth has emerged to fashion the reality of a rock-suckled cohort group.

Rock is class conscious and democratic; it is elitist and leveling. Both contradictory comments are true. For the music is dynamic, inventing new contexts within which to celebrate its appeal. It is "chewing gum for the mind," and it is artful. And it is so because it has made rational thought mythic.

There are, of course, many levels on which to evaluate

meaning. The one I have chosen to stress here is the result of the music, its effect on generational views. Yet here too there are significant nuances: The Presley fans who hate Roy Orbison; the Beatle admirers who detest the Stones; Dylan freaks who find "new wave" incomprehensible. The list goes on to the very core of the music. Then there is the intention of a song—its style and rhythm—and its lyric. The former is intuitive, relying on basic, primordial feelings—to some extent cut off from convention; the latter is rational, depending on thought or repetition for its message to sink in.

The meaning of rock is unquestionably linked to the cultural life of this nation. It is our product, the way automobiles and refrigerators and wrapped bread are our products. Now it belongs to everyone. Its meaning has Americanized the globe.

We stand at the beginning of a new age, searching for answers about our past and hoping to get a glimpse of the future. But our vision is hazy. We require a compass or some clue that may put us back in familiar territory. Rock music and the response to it can provide that barometer of social change.

It is my belief that, if one assumes that the last four decades have been revolutionary, resulting in a challenge to sensibilities infinitely more extreme than those occurring during many political revolutions, then rock music is the medium used to convey social change. It is also assumed that, since the music is inextricably tied to this revolutionary history, rock lyrics are compatible with the history of the era. Some social historians may not take this claim seriously, but I believe rock music is an archivist's wish fulfilled. I intend to prove that rock parallels this revolution of sensibilities and so gives us unique insights into our recent history.

Crane Brinton, in *The Anatomy of Revolution* (1938), argued that past revolutions (four in particular—English, French, American, and Russian) went through discernible stages of development. Admittedly these were political revolutions whose goals were generally pragmatic—a change in leadership. Yet there were the ideas that inspired political change—naive, adolescent, culturally "progressive," passionate, and always idealistic ideas. Saint Just made no distinction between good and bad, heaven and hell; "There is only desire." "Experience!" he cried.

> I want to live henceforth in my own way
> To defy, flatter, speak, be silent, laugh
> To love, to hate.

> I shall speak of all peoples, of all religions,
> of all laws as if I myself did not adhere to any. . . .
> *I detach myself* from everything in order to attach
> myself to everything.*

Jerry Rubin said, "Do it!"; Abbie Hoffman urged the young to "do what you want to do." Two hundred years had passed, but the torch of revolution continued to burn in language that was faintly reminiscent of what had been said many times before. Nietzsche described it as "the weariness that wants to reach the ultimate with one leap. . . ." That is the revolutionary's vision. He wants to start again, to wipe the slate clean, to have before him a *tabula rasa* on which to draw a "new man." It is glib, but also accurate, to describe the last four decades as a revolution with remarkable cultural victories and overwhelming political defeats. That *tabula*

---

*Quoted in James H. Billington, *Fire in the Minds of Men* (New York: Basic Books, 1980), pp. 64, 65.

rasa has not been discovered, but this revolution has left its mark on several generations whose perceptions of morality and culture are immutably altered. This cultural revolution is deliberately obscure. But at a minimum it includes unrepressed sensuality, a contempt for ordinary categories of rational thought and speech, rejection of organized work, support for the avant garde in art, a search for personal fulfillment divorced from conventions, and a fascination with areas of thought stigmatized by prevailing social sentiments—e.g., pornography, drugs. In its most debased forms, it is represented by those who oppose any discipline and who regard it as a badge of revolutionary commitment to flaunt their hedonism, their lack of loyalty to any institution, and their intellectual ignorance.

Of course, this cultural approach invites political failure. How can a revolution succeed without discipline and sacrifice? How can sexual freedom occur when liberty can't be guaranteed? Puritans make revolution, not hedonists.

Yet something did happen; something fundamentally different from the past has occurred. The upper middle class, rooted in the media events of the age, fell in love with the idea of a sudden break with the past, a break with compromise, concessions, adjustments to memory, selfishness, stupidity, and barren traditions. For a moment it appeared in this new dawn as if all things were possible. Like Shelley's magic words, ''The world's great age begins anew,'' a revolution undermining the social and cultural order did occur. A society based on custom, cues, and manners was forced to see its traditional order dissolve. The serpent was let loose in Eden and, as recent events suggest, he is not easily tamed.

The cultural life of the present is not like that of the prewar era. Nudity can now be seen in every movie house in this land and almost everywhere in the free world. Marijuana has become so commonplace that one can hardly pass a park in our major cities where it is not being used; pornography of the most blatant variety masquerades as art; family deterioration has become a national epidemic; standards of right and wrong have retreated before the onslaught of relativism and consciousness raising. Something happened, and if it isn't revolution, it sure has fooled me.

This revolution—I assert—is very much like its predecessors. It has gone through the standard stages: incipient change; reform; active revolt; equilibrium; reaction; and restoration. If the respondents to my queries about rock have different reactions to the music that mirrors this history, the variation is due in large measure to the point at which this dynamic music had its greatest impact on their lives. In a sense, the musical tastes reflect a moment in the development of this revolutionary history. Like the inscriptions on the Rosetta stone that solved the mystery of hieroglyphics, rock music provides a key record of the Second American Revolution that may unlock its inner logic. But I do not wish to overstate the case. Rock is a spectator at the cultural storm, not its ruler. It may rekindle the ashes with a spark, but it cannot make the original fire.

If this book has a specific goal it is to explore the relationship between rock music and the society that nurtured it. Arthur Schlesinger Jr. has written, ''The unique subject matter for the intellectual historian is the role thought plays in enabling men and women to accept and transform their environment. The unifying focus is the problem of how and why people change their minds.'' Rock music doesn't explain it all, but it is a marvelous vehicle of transmission, a way of conveying ideas. That is what I hope to illustrate in the chapters that follow.

TWO

THE ANCIEN REGIME

*I*n my view the period between the era of bebop and mid-fifties rock was the *ancien regime* of popular music. It was a time of relative musical equilibrium. Nonintellectual taste gravitated to "Deep in the Heart of Texas," "White Christmas," "Don't Fence Me In," "How Much Is That Doggie in the Window?" and "Secret Love." The "sweetness and light" (to borrow a phrase from Matthew Arnold) united intellectuals—loosely speaking—writers, artists, and musicians—with a feeling that this appearance of social equilibrium, brought about by the war effort, had created a new national ethos, one dominated by acceptance of the social and cultural status quo. It was almost as if this view represented an established opinion, albeit below the surface was a music of profound uneasiness with the social order.

Jazz, blues, and country had always been the language of the alienated—including the discontented intellectual elite. The jazz was nonconformist, the blues had searing emotions, and country gave you the sentiment of down-home folk. Muddy Waters sang about worry, dissatisfaction and tears in the night. A revolutionary musical myth was fashioned out of the symbols of subterranean sounds. Presumably the music of black suffering, experimental lyrics, pure sensuality, and unrequited love had a message. It was a genuine cry of real people rather than the manufactured pabulum of Tin Pan Alley. Moreover, it was believed that this music was conceived by a sense of dissatisfaction, unfolding in a conviction that what is, not only ought not, but need not, be.

For many adolescents in this war/postwar era the energy of blues and jazz seemed to suggest a new era of equality and justice—rhetorical words that ignored both the contradictions and complexity they suggest. These "sounds of the people" would bring us together—white and black, urban and rural poor, lower and middle classes. It is often suggested that the music "caused" revolutionary thought and action. Of course this chicken-and-egg hypothesis is futile to pursue. Did the music cause certain conditions, or is it a reflection of conditions? It is probably both. Specific social problems elicit a musical response, which in turn reinforces public attitudes. Music, particularly folk music, tends to focus on a better world, and in the abstract, those conditions that might actually bring about a better world. In this sense, it is the expression of ideas that makes music revolutionary—a necessary albeit insufficient cause for revolution. After all, music is decorative. In its ineffable form, it blankets real motives and ideas. Yet it is—sometimes despite itself— reflective of a trend. When the young of my generation sang "Hail, rock 'n' roll," the curtain was falling on the past, and the vague yearnings of a new era found a means for expression.

For much of our history, black music (rhythm and blues), jazz, and folk were largely ignored by the bulk of the population. There were, of course, always aficionados, but it was considered slumming to be in Storytown, New Orleans, or at the Cotton Club in Harlem. The seeming exclusivity of this music suggested that the "message" was different from what the rest of America usually heard.

The black gospel singing in the South was mysterious and, as a consequence, sometimes threatening. Its shuddering rhythms and evocative beat were faintly familiar to an American audience that by the thirties had imbibed the sanitized ragtime of Irving Berlin and the syncopated black rhythms of Whiteman and Goodman. But this was undiluted backcountry music that hypnotized black congregants with its repetitive style. It was generally not understood, and so it was easily dismissed. Yet its influence is unmistakable.

Among music buffs it has become fashionable to discuss a fusion of sounds, styles, rhythms, and lyrics. Since music is created by both witting and unwitting melodic kleptomaniacs, it is impossible to know who should get credit for what. This, however, does not dampen the spirit of music archaeologists who dig beneath the surface to find musical fossils that provide hints about provenance. Their efforts occasionally pay off, particularly for those who want to know if the Graves Brothers' record "Barbecue Bust" (1936) is related to the spiritual "Run Old Jeremiah," or who wonder about some other instance of musical exotica. Yet that misses the point. The music is distinctly evolutionary, almost—but not quite—a seamless web combining rural farm songs with religious spirituals and urban sounds.

Rock 'n' roll was the musical outgrowth of this hybridization. Hillbillies—who were affected by black music—mixed rural blues, banjo melodies, and church music to create something unique (the country-and-western genre). But the

story of rock is ostensibly the imprint of black music on
white America, with all that suggests. The musical roots go
back to Africa, but the lyrical origins are related to the black
experience with oppression in this land. From an authentic
bluesman like Blind Lemon Jefferson to the mandolinist Bill
Monroe, who some describe as the father of bluegrass, the
music emphasized a driving rhythm of a movement "in the
air." It was impossible to give it a name or be specific, but as
the intellectuals discussed social change and civil rights, the
beat became heavier and more insistent. In a sense, music
was the social Cassandra speaking in a language that few
could really understand.

A Cappella
Eddie Chamblee Interview, February 17, 1982

Bands around school started doing our own little inventions
in blues. We had a certain beat that we developed into rock
and roll. Horns, saxophones and guitars were the principal
instruments in it. Around Chicago at that time, that's where
I'm from, there were a lot of guys from down South, you
know. Muddy Waters, Blue Willie, Crazy John, Big Black
Sam. We sort of made a juxtaposition between our swing and
their blues. That was sort of the beginning of my association
with rock. In those years I formed a band because I had to
make a living. I made a few records out of Chicago. And
some of them were pretty big hits. One of them was "Long
Gone Blues," which was a transition of the old blues of the
Louis Armstrong style into a new swinging version. My association, my roots, are with the King Curtis band who, inci-
dentally, imitated me on its first hit records.

When an Eddie Durham recorded the first solos with the
new electric guitar in 1938, the instrument of modern musi-

cal revolution was discovered. In 1939 Charlie Christian recorded for Benny Goodman with an electric guitar, followed in turn by T. Bone Walker, who was the musical bridge between the blues and Chuck Berry's rock guitar style. Yet there were many roads leading to rock music. Jazz bands with a boogie-woogie rhythm such as Louis Jordan's were recording tunes that had a profound influence on rock. Bill Doggett, a lead performer and arranger with the Jordan band, and then Lionel Hampton, Count Basie, and Louis Armstrong went on to make the sensational rock hit, "Honky Tonk," in 1956. Little Willie Littlefield's "K. C. Living," a well-known jazz tune, became the inspiration for the Leiber and Stoller hit "Kansas City" recorded by Wilbert Harrison in 1959. And blues singers like Muddy Waters and Howlin' Wolf were direct descendants of Fats Domino.

A Cappella
Bill Doggett Interview, October 28, 1981

Many jazz tunes were real rock hits, like "Night Train," Jimmy Forrest's "Night Train." Here you have a great solo, great tenor saxophonist, but it, the rhythm, is so simple. You don't think of "Night Train" as a jazz tune written by Jimmy Forrest, but that's what he wrote it for. It's a rock tune, it's rhythm and blues. You can remember that. The minute you go into it, you know it. Simple tunes and basic chords, that's what rock is about. Because I can remember, and I guess I am as much to blame for this as anybody else. When we were coming along in the early forties, when the bebopping stuff came along, we were trying to do all kinds of things with chords. We started adding ninths and flat fifths and all this other stuff, and we lost the public. The public is not interested in listening to flat fifths and raised thirds, minor sevenths, they are interested in what feels and what hears good to them.

Younger people are always going to want to move, the energy and everything. They like the ballads and things, but basically they want the beat. Let me tell you how "Honky Tonk" got started. "Honky Tonk" was a mistake. We hadn't ever played anything like that before until we had gotten into Lima, Ohio, early in 1956. We were playing a Sunday night dance, and we got in there at about four or five o'clock in the afternoon. We were playing pool in the afternoon, we had something to eat. A couple of guys went into the bar and had a couple of tastes. So, out of the clear blue sky we played maybe a half hour and all of a sudden, just out of nowhere, Billy Butler started playing this thing but we didn't know what he was going to do—whether he was going to play it all or just end it—so we just sat there patiently and listened until we discovered it was going to be a blues tune. In the meantime, Billy had played four or five bars or so and then it got to the third change. Now it seemed to lend itself to a shuffle rhythm, so I started playing the shuffle to the blues. We had a rule in the band—not a rule, a formula—that if Billy started a tune, then Scotty (Clifford Scott) would play after Billy, and I would play after Scotty. If I played the first sixteen bars, then Scotty would play, and then Billy. Well, on this night Billy improvised and we all joined in. The crowd loved it. They were dancin' all over the place. When it was over, we went on to another tune. But that audience said, play that other one again. Damn, I didn't know whether Billy could do it. But he did. He played that song fifteen straight times that night. We really turned 'em on. When we got home I got us into a studio and put that sound on a record. That's how "Honky Tonk" was born. It was all luck, and it turned out to be one of the great rock hits of all time.

After World War II there was an irresistible desire for more musical experimentation on the part of an intellectual elite. This was the period of the Beats, who wanted to hear a rocking boogie beat that would drown out the existential conformity they so deplored. Joe Turner and his pianist Pete Johnson, along with Meade Lux Lewis and Albert Ammons, became an underground musical revolution for those who liked their music hot. In short order this music was subsumed into Tommy Dorsey hits like "Boogie Woogie," the Andrews Sisters' "Boogie Woogie Bugle Boy," and Ernie Ford's "Shotgun Boogie."

Rhythm and blues went through several incarnations until a Western swing musician named Bill Haley and his group, the Saddlemen, later called the Comets, applied the "rocking" sound of Ike Turner's "Rocket '88" to their record "Rock the Joint" (1952). Haley may have been among the first, but he was by no means the only white performer to "cover" black records. In 1954 the Crew-Cuts' version of the Chords' "Sh-Boom" was the most successful song of the year. The lyric was early Tin Pan Alley with the inclusion of some thinly secularized gospel music.

> Life could be a dream
> If you will take me up to paradise up above,
> If you will tell me I'm the only one that you love
> Life can be a dream sweetheart
> Hey nonny ding dang alang, alang, alang.

A year later Haley recorded "Rock Around the Clock," which quickly became number one on the pop charts, due undoubtedly to its inclusion in the film *Blackboard Jungle*. What isn't widely known is that Haley had imbibed and used the Southern rhythm-and-blues style of Joe Turner for his hit and later went on to cover Turner's "Shake, Rattle and Roll."

By 1956 the era of rock 'n' roll was in full bloom. Chuck Berry, Fats Domino, and Little Richard were already on the pop charts. And looming over the entire decade was the shadow of the young Elvis Presley. Presley had been weaned on country music and rhythm and blues by Sam Phillips, the producer at Sun Records and his early mentor. But he was very much a product of his environment. The Mississippi blues singer Arthur "Big Boy" Crudup had his influence, as did Carl Perkins, whose hit "Blue Suede Shoes" Presley later recorded, and of course, Otis Blackwell. Since young Presley was a church-attending Baptist, his earliest musical influence was gospel music. He said, "Since I was two years old all I knew was gospel music; that was music to me." Presley was in no sense a revolutionary by nature. He was a religious, conservative, polite, diffident man who could "ma'am" and "sir" his way into the hearts of his elders at an early age and inspire chills in adolescents as he got older.

What lifted Presley into the revolutionary spotlight was his unconventional style. That sneer, his whole attitude, exemplified the scornful indifference of James Dean, his idol, or the young Marlon Brando in *The Wild One*. His was the style of playful irreverence, a style that appealed to the young who were dissatisfied with conformity, yet not sure of how to express nonconformity. That this ostensibly self-effacing young man should so well reflect the rebellious character of a generation about to shatter the norms of its parents is one of the great ironies of our time. In fact—without relying too heavily on psychological speculation—I think it could be suggested that Presley's subsequent torment was due to his being caught in the maelstrom of social change, indeed being the focus of youthful rebellion, when his own nature and instincts were rooted in the maintenance of tradition. What greater irony than that this figure of youthful idolatry should spend his last years in Las Vegas singing "Lawdy Miss Clawdy" to middle-aged audiences as he sought peace from the world in a vial filled with tranquilizers.

In so many ways Presley was the twentieth-century Figaro. After all, it was the operatic Figaro who told his master Count Almaviva that the times were changing, that the prevailing values would not stand. Presley captured the same spirit, although like most early revolutionaries he was probably unaware of what he represented and perplexed by his power to sway opinions. He didn't organize his music to change the world—he was loyal to the memories of the past—but the Presley style was a metaphor that spoke volumes to the sentiments of the young. This rock revolution was in every sense a surprise, as Presley was a surprising symbol. Yet, for the symbol to emerge as it did, there had to be something in the air, a Zeitgeist congenial to this new musical sound.

I would argue that the external conditions of life bring about changes internally. What people find they can do in society influences their perception of themselves. Music evokes this interior self. Without relying on scientific data to support this contention, I believe one can cite music as a force for human awareness. It also conspires with the other arts to create a social consciousness. It weaves emotion around events and human relationships until a language and form evolve. This theory does not deny the objective dimension of music; it is merely an effort to understand how a new social and personal awareness may develop as an audience shares the world view of an artist. Through the experience of music, people may discover a new common thread that knits them together and thus develop a feeling of kinship with one another. This—as much as the music itself—is why the rock concert emerged as a social form and why the inner and very personal songs of the early rock performers had such a profound social impact.

What distinguishes rock from other musical forms is its eclecticism. The music is dynamic—forever changing, responding, evolving. If it is anything, it is impressionistic. The lyrics sometimes have hidden meanings; the melody may be little more than a vague concatenation of sound. Listening to rock is like watching a Monet painting. If you stand too close, it's a blur; too far away, it loses detail. But at the right distance, there is always more to be seen. Perhaps that explains why rock is so hard for the social scientist to explain. If one relies entirely on the words for analysis, the real meaning of rock is lost. Yet how does one attribute meaning to ineffable sound? Greil Marcus said it best, I believe, with his enigmatic claim that "words are sounds we can feel before they are statements to understand." We are dealing here with the world of feelings and senses, and in a true ethnographic sense rock is tribalism. There is an obvious paradox: I do evaluate lyrics because they cannot be dismissed, but I recognize full well that they are only part of a complex story whose illumination is dependent on transcendent characteristics.

Music is obviously more than notes and words strung together. Socrates actually warned against the playing of several musical modes and passages of poetry that could potentially disturb the delicate balance in the body politic. "Never are the ways of music moved," Socrates said, "without the greatest political laws being moved." In the soul of the state,

"good harmony . . . and good rhythm accompany good dis-
position." Socrates was prescient. Since music doesn't depend on understanding, the power being in its sensual force,
there is no rational antidote to it. A social meaning appears
inherently in music's structure. Karl Marx taught that music
has concrete meaning in the midst of abstractions. And the
totalitarian spirit of any stripe respects, fears, and attempts
to control the musical form. Rock is no different from its an-
cestry on this matter, except that it may be an even more extreme challenge to prevailing sentiments than the music of
the past. It did pose a threat to contemporary standards, and
it does move listeners. Through such conditions a social system is changed.

Shadows of My Mind
Look, June 26, 1956

Going to a rock 'n' roll show is like attending the rites of
some obscure tribe whose means of communication are incomprehensible. An adult can actually be frightened. Two
notes are played on-stage and, like one vast organism, the
assembled teen-agers shriek on exactly the same pitch. Or,
just as suddenly, they become deathly quiet except for the
rhythmic clapping of their hands on the second and fourth
beat of every measure. Another number is played, and, like
one voice, they sing, "Why-iey do foo-ools fall in lu-
uve?"—their youthful enunciation and melody somehow
sweet and haunting. Sometimes, a few of them dance—in the
aisles if there is no other place. More rarely, they engage in
more strenuous exhibitionism.

In 1956 (June 18) a *Time* magazine editor wrote that rock
music "does for music what a motorcycle club at full throttle
does for a quiet Sunday afternoon." He cited as its central

characteristics "an unrelenting, socking syncopation that sounds like a bull whip; a choleric saxophone honking mating call sounds; an electric guitar turned up so loud that its sound shatters and splits; a vocal group that shudders and exercises violently to the beat while roughly chanting either a near-nonsense phrase or a moronic lyric in hillbilly idiom."

What the author of this statement didn't mention, but what was most apparent to any listener in the early fifties, is rock's most obvious feature: sexuality. The race music of the forties and fifties was a celebration of sex through suggestive words, i.e. "jelly," "rider," "movin'." But that intense, direct beat also had an emotional effect that moralists quite rightly perceived as a threat to respectable behavior. For teens who formerly made public compromises so that their private views could remain intact, here was a music that permitted public expression of introspective rebellion. This was Stendhalian thought turned outward.

> LONG TALL SALLY
> Long tall Sally has a lot on the ball
> Nobody cares if she's long and tall
> Oh, Baby! Yeh-heh-heh-heh, Baby
> Whoo-oo-oo-oo, Baby! I'm havin' me
> some fun tonight, yeah."

Said an Oakland, California, policeman, after watching Elvis Presley, "If he did that in the street, we'd arrest him" (*Time*, May 14, 1956). Asa Carter, a representative of the White Citizens Council of Alabama said "there was a plot to mongrelize America. Rock 'n' roll," he argued, "appeals to the base in man, brings out animalism and vulgarity" (*Newsweek*, April 23, 1956). Frank Sinatra was quoted in the *New York Times* (January 12, 1958) as having said that

"Rock 'n' roll smells phony and false. It is sung, played and written for the most part by cretinous goons and by means of its almost imbecilic reiteration and sly, lewd, in plain fact, dirty lyrics . . . manages to be the martial music of every side-burned delinquent on the face of the earth." A. D. Buchmueller, a psychiatric social worker and executive director of the Child Study Association, said, "Kids, just like adults, get caught up in a mass kind of hysteria, which is contagious. Some get hurt by it physically and emotionally" (*New York Times*, January 12, 1958). And the same issue of the *New York Times* quoted Judge Hilda Schwartz as saying, "What a pity that . . . this yearning for something and someone to look up to, this outpouring of energy and love should have been concentrated on a fad that can only be a passing interest."

Passing interest, indeed. "Rock 'n' roll is here to stay, it will never die," was the rejoinder to comments like that. Regardless of where one stood on the rock controversy of the early fifties, there was no denying the vitality of the music. Rock music helped to give birth to an ideology of adolescence. While the adolescent has always felt like an outcast, trapped between the worlds of childhood innocence and adult maturity, there had been no true means of expressing such fears and concerns. It is not a coincidence that white adolescents from the fifties and early sixties borrowed black music for their ideology, since the black was isolated from the cultural mainstream in the way adolescents perceived themselves to be. Just as the black felt that music was one way to express his frustration with racism, white adolescents turned to this music as a form of rebellion against cultural norms that seemed to ignore them. In fact, the ideology became so pervasive that by the late sixties it was no longer bound by age—"extended adolescence" meant in effect that anyone could be a teenager. Embracing rock music was one way to ensure this condition. Rock wasn't a fountain of youth, but it did provide illusions.

A Cappella
Frank Zappa Interview, November 18, 1981

Well, my favorite era of rock music was the fifties, especially the years 1955 to 1958. The downfall of the original rock 'n' roll form came when smart-ass producers started adding violins to everything, and that ruined it. The rhythm and blues records that were made in fifty-five generally went down in quality after fifty-eight. Those were the ones that I liked the best. That is the bulk of my album collection. Because I believe that music was sincere and melodious and free. It had a sense of humor to it and sounded like it was made by people for the enjoyment of other people, as opposed to a product made by companies for the amusement of a mass audience. In those days there were sincere songs about a guy's girlfriend. Whether you liked the girlfriend or not is beside the point. How the guy who would seriously sing you a song felt was clear. That's the way it was, you could really identify with it. That was the golden age as far as I am concerned.

The "hip style" of the late fifties was based on the adolescent assumption that the only way to cope with the world was to drop out. "If people don't recognize the insanity of nuclear war or that apocalypse is around the corner, I'm not going to tell them. I'll just get my kicks while I can. Life gets shorter every day, I mean, man, the only worthwhile thing is in myself. Anything else is a drag" (*New Republic,* April 21, 1958). So was delivered the adolescent address, the one that presaged the Me Generation, the one that ultimately rode the Eden Express to disaster, and the one that opened the Pandora's box of adolescent drug abuse.

This second American revolution—based on changing manners and morals—was led by faddish teenagers who were inarticulate, self-absorbed, and massaged by the rock sounds that awakened their sensibilities to a new group experience. As is the case in all revolutions, the supporters pointed to their moral superiority, the detractors to the unscrupulous character of the opposition. However, revolutionists, in order to stay in power, gloss over their personal victory and attempt to create a general feeling of victory, one in which resistance to the new authority is somehow illegitimate. So it was with rock. The musical revolution that had borrowed from the blues, country, and street sounds now had grafted on to it the voice of protest. As the net was spread, the opposition was subsumed into the national trend, wondering why there had been so much hoopla surrounding the music in the first place.

A Cappella
Kal Rudman Interview, September 28, 1981

The history of the revolution in music started with radio. When the war baby boom hit its peak—1955—radio stations were being smashed to smithereens by television, which was coming out of its cocoon, and becoming a mammoth butterfly from an ugly caterpillar. The country had been wired, TV was set up, we had color coming in and everybody owned the hardware [owned the set]. You've got to remember about owning the hardware; before you start with the aesthetics and the esoterics, you start with the pragmatics. You start with the hardware. All of a sudden people were buying record players. RCA did a phenomenal promotion. For $35 you got a self-contained 45 [rpm] record player. For sixteen bucks you got a unit which you could plug into any speaker. So now for the first time they had mass-marketed the hardware and they could sell their 45's.

You had a bunch of failing radio stations (AM of course), many of them on the far right-hand side of the dial with weak signals, whose programming was foreign language or ethnic. The first thing that happened was that black stations came in and took over the foreign language stations; e.g., Philadelphia's WDAS, which was always foreign language, switched on black programming. It first started in the late forties and early fifties and had been there as an undercurrent. It was an explosion waiting to detonate; it just needed the right combination of the various components for these media vehicles to penetrate the mass consciousness of the United States. You had country, you had blues waiting to coalesce into something called rock 'n' roll. At about that time the Ertegun brothers hired Jerry Wexler from *Billboard* and really got the Atlantic Records thing going. It was a legitimately run firm. They paid legitimate royalties, did not rip anybody off; in fact, paid royalties upfront. There were many rhythm-and-blues labels. I used to call them Seventh Avenue Rhythm and Blues. You had a guitar, an electric bass, a bass drum. A guy "tripped" over the guitar into the bass drum and you had instant soul on Seventh Avenue in New York City. These groups were really cocktail-lounge acts, but then it got to the point where record companies really had to start delivering hits.

The first R 'n' R hit was "Gee" by the Crows on the Gone/ End label owned by the late George Goldner. Nobody really knows that it was a B side and it was played by an all-night disc jockey in LA, who did his show in a storefront window. I didn't even know what the name of the A side was. The independent record distributor told the record company that they had a hit and ordered 10,000. The "Sh'boom" by the Chords, which was really rhythm and blues, was recorded and was covered by a white act, the Crew Cuts. The Chords' "Sh'boom" really took off in fifty-four. It really exploded! The DJs caught on that this was really the way to go. You had this vast untapped audience, because pop music then was bleached-out white-bread music. White pop was set up for the kill, like lambs waiting to be sent to the slaughter. They went for something new and exciting. They went to a "new" music they could relate to. There's no difference between the appeal of doo wop in New York City and New Wave in New York City. It's the same kids, nothing has changed. There have been no mutations, no genetic aberrations, no chromosomal debacles. They need high-energy music as an outlet for their energy. They want simplistic words and love themes that befit their psychology and mentality.

Rock music had to be cultivated in a congenial soil by gardeners committed to its fruition. The music had authentic roots in the experience of its performers. It was often tasteless and simple, but it was always exuberant—a genuine expression of despair or, as Charlie Gillett, has put it, *The Sounds of the City*. This, in part, explains why some aficionados describe early rock as sincere and its later forms as inauthentic or manufactured (see Simon Frith, *The Sociology of Rock,* chapter 11). Both the Marxists—who are convinced that rock is a form of social control to keep the masses intoxicated with an orgiastic beat—and the musical elitists—who view rock as degrading and puerile—underestimate its cultural influence.

It is instructive that in the mid-fifties attitudes towards rock music were a litmus test for teenage attitudes generally.

In my social circle you had to like "Hold Em Joe" by Harry
Belafonte or feel rejection. As a bona fide Coasters freak, I
thought Belafonte had as much to say to me as Arthur God-
frey. The Coasters were speaking a language—admittedly
simple—that represented my pent-up feelings. In a curious
way, they were utopians of the street. It often seemed to me
that being rejected for liking music of the masses was like
being rejected for admiring democracy. Although the parallels seem farfetched, music that is an expression of grass-
roots sentiments has cultural meaning even when—and perhaps especially because—it offends the prevailing norms of
"good music." Admittedly, exploitation of that authentic
expression took place in the form of manufactured sounds
that had little to do with music and a lot to do with technology. But that is a later stage in the revolutionary cycle.

Notwithstanding the Marxist perspective, rock enhanced
the social basis for cultural struggle in the mid-fifties. David
Riesman's *The Lonely Crowd* and William Whyte's *The Organization Man* created the impression that mass society had
arrived, that conformity was the inexorable response to this
new social order. Joseph McCarthy—however much he as a
symbol has been abused—stood for conformity in the face of
iconoclastic positions.

The view of the culture as conformist may have been over-
stated, but early rock music was a visible retreat from conformity. The music didn't impose an ideology on a youthful
subculture—if anything, it absorbed latent values and gave
them back to a receptive audience as a new symbol. Almost
unwittingly the music became the focus of a counterculture. I
use the phrase "almost unwittingly" because the primary
goal of musical producers was not to foment social change;
yet anyone close to the music knew what kind of feelings and

experiences were being unleashed. Murray the K said, "You couldn't be close to the music and not know something was happening. I wasn't sure of what it was in the fifties, but when I saw kids dancin' in the aisles at the Fox, I knew there was a lot of energy there."

Perhaps the clearest and most authentic expression of this energy was in what was once called the "doo wop" sound. Kenny Vance, who sang with Jay and the Americans, described it accurately as "Looking for an Echo." Here were the street kids of the city looking for a small space between two city buildings where in *a cappella* fashion they could harmonize to nonsensical syllables. This was pure New York City rock of the fifties based on urban black vocal harmony transmogrified into Italian, Puerto Rican, and Jewish alley sounds.

While black vocal harmony has antecedents that go back centuries, rock owes a very significant debt to the Ink Spots, particularly the Spots of pre-1944 (before the extraordinary bass Orville "Hoppy" Jones died). Renditions of "If I Didn't Care" and "My Prayer," with Bill Kenny singing lead, were the inspirational force for a livelier and more gospel-laden sound of the Drifters and the Platters ten years later. The Orioles' "Crying in the Chapel" (1953) has the same rhythmic beat as "If I Didn't Care"; and the Crows' "Gee" (1954), often considered the first rock record (albeit there are many who disagree with that claim), had a lead singer who imitated Clyde McPhatter, who was imitating Bill Kenny.

In 1954 the Penguins—a group from Los Angeles— recorded "Earth Angel" (Dootone Records), which because of its success became a model for rock 'n' roll melodies over the next ten years. The song had all the trappings of "doo

wop'' harmony plus a simple romanticism well expressed by
lead singer Cleve Duncan.

> Earth Angel, Earth Angel
> Will you be mine?
> Oh darling dear, love you all the time.
> I'm just a fool, a fool in love with you oo oo oo.

The following year "Story Untold" was recorded by the
Nutmegs, and a year after that came "Why Do Fools Fall in
Love" by Frankie Lyman and the Teenagers. By this point
"toom-a-toom-a-toom," "oodly-pop-a-cow-cow," "byip,
byip, byip," and "sha-na-na" all had emerged as prominent
and well-recognized sounds on the records of early rock. It is
hard to believe that "shoo-doo-shoo-be-doo" would be the
inchoate call of revolution; yet curiously it captured an adolescent penchant for independence through a language that
was intentionally absurd, strangely hypnotic, and idiosyn-
cratically youthful.

What Robert Christgau and Greil Marcus suggest about
rock music as a "source of solidarity," a symbol of community, was certainly true of early rock. It was the voice of adolescence and the religion of an adolescent subculture. In a
casual way, rock captured the repressed concerns of adolescents generally; but, in another sense, rock was a form of
countercultural statement for admirers of "Rebel Without a
Cause."

The language of incoherent simplicisms was like the egali-
tarian language of revolution in the 1780s. Rock songs
weren't thoughtfully written; they were the effort of playful
passion. Yet that passion produced an irreverence, and the
irreverence produced an iconoclasm. Before the outbreak of
revolution in 1789, small groups of trusted friends would

meet in Paris cafes to discuss unconventional ideas, engage in hedonistic pleasures, and listen to music that was novel to the ear. André Monglond wrote, "there is no scene . . . which did not end in tears and embraces." A circle of people with shared values evolved into a unit for revolutionary activity. In a curiously similar way, the circle of rock adherents—those who embraced the style of rock—shared inner thoughts through the music and formed a strength from the uniformity of those ideas, which formed an emergent ideology. Because of such social circles, the Ancien Regime fell in 1789 and once again a century and a half later.

THREE

THE CONFORMIST YEARS

When rock music made its first appearance on radio in the fifties, I felt enraptured by what I heard. I couldn't wait to retreat into my world of Alan Freed and Moondog. The sounds turned Patti Page from my teenage heartthrob into the female counterpart of Caspar Milquetoast. How could those saccharine sounds in "Tennessee Waltz" possibly compare to the rhythmic beat in the Penguins' "Earth Angel"?

Yet my perceptions were based on the musical sounds, not the lyrics. While rock music at the beginning was considered a threat to morality and conventions, its lyrics more often than not reflected the values of adult authority. Perhaps what many adults found objectionable was its style—Presley's pelvic movement, Berry's phallic guitar, the Big Bopper's sexy incantations—since they never heard the words. But for me who was glued to WINS and listened intently to every word, every "shu be du," the message was clear: conformity to material standards and accepted moral conventions ensured my dream of "success and happiness."

Yet in the pages of Charles Reich's *The Greening of Amer-*

ica, Richard Goldstein's *The Poetry of Rock,* and Jonathan Eisen's *The Age of Rock,* these songs were considered protest music, a source of youthful rebellion. And in one sense these critics were right. That beat had a narcotic effect. It is also accurate to assert that, at a certain point in this revolutionary history, the lyrics caught up to the musical revolution. But there was a significant lag. Listening to rock in the mid-fifties, I heard a defense of prosperity, consumerism, contracts, institutional loyalty, power, and reason. But I may have been one of the very few who were actually listening to the words.

During this period (the second stage of revolution) rock 'n' roll was an unorthodox musical sound, with strange characters and approaches to the presentation of a song. But it was not yet a medium for assaulting traditions through its lyrics. What it did—with startling success—was stimulate a youthful crowd with an obsessive rhythmical beat that had them dancing in the aisles. It was the physical response of the listener that challenged prevailing conventions.

Shadows of My Mind
Time, June 18, 1955

In Boston Roman Catholic leaders urged that the offensive music be boycotted. In Hartford city officials considered revoking the State Theater's license after several audiences got too rowdy during a musical stage show. In Washington the police chief recommended banning such shows from the National Guard Armory after brawls in which several people were injured. In Minneapolis a theater manager withdrew a film featuring the music after a gang of youngsters left the theater, snake-danced around town and smashed windows. In Birmingham champions of white supremacy decried it as part of a Negro plot against the whites. At a wild concert in Atlanta's baseball park one night, fists and beer bottles were thrown, four youngsters were arrested.

The object of all this attention is a musical style known as "rock 'n' roll," which has captivated U.S. adolescents as swing captivated prewar teenagers and ragtime vibrated those of the '20s. Rock 'n' roll is based on Negro blues, but in a self-conscious style which underlines the primitive qualities of the blues with malice aforethought. Characteristics: an unrelenting socking syncopation—that sounds like a bull whip; a choleric saxophone honking mating-call sounds; an electric guitar turned up so loud that its sound shatters and splits; a vocal group that shudders and exercises violently to the beat while roughly chanting either a near-nonsense phrase or a moronic lyric in hillbilly idiom.

R. Serge Denisoff argued—quite rightly I believe—that folk music attempted to inculcate a political consciousness, but popular music, including early rock, was viewed as "a tool of the bourgeoisie." He maintained in an article entitled "Proletarian Renascence" that it wasn't until the 1960s, "when middle class intellectuals discarded their backgrounds to become working class," that Tin Pan Alley altered its adherence to traditional values. This squares with my own experience. When I was a teenager, it was the Harry Belafonte and Folk City freaks who wore jeans and had a rather snobbish and revolutionary attitude about music. For those of us who loved the Coasters and Frankie Lyman, it was V-neck sweaters, white bucks, chinos, and a clean cut. Revolution was for world history, not my history, and the music I listened to was for jivin', not telling people how to beat "the system."

It has always been my opinion that early rock songs provided a language appropriate for the social roles articulated by television programs and motion pictures for the fifties. Keep in mind that Howdy Doody was the ultimate conformist; in his confrontations with Clarabelle, the potential revolutionary, he always won. Similarly, Sandra Dee may not have liked her parents' rigid rules, but in every film, after several bad experiences she came to realize Mom and Dad had been right all along.

A Cappella
Murray the K, Interview, September 30, 1981

The influence rock 'n' roll had on our society was due to the fact that television made young people better informed, better able to judge their parents' standards and being educated to what's really going on. They absolutely craved something that could be their own, something that the parents couldn't share, and certainly it wasn't property or real things, it was music. Rock was just a new expression which reflected a belief that the younger people did not accept society as it was laying down the laws of what you can do and what you can't do. There was a revolution taking place; it's always the young people who have the energy to start something. The media gave strength to the feelings that were perhaps dormant within a lot of young people until R&R was born, and as it started to proceed there was something about the music—a 2 or $2\frac{1}{2}$ minute song communicating immediately. The music spread like wildfire, and it was revolutionary indeed, because most of the people, the establishment, as it were, people who couldn't understand the music, were afraid of it, put it down, barred it, and the more there was an objection to it, the more the young people took to it, as theirs. They changed their mode of dress, their hair, the attitude they had about certain things, social standards. They changed even the way they danced. They tried to break away from the generation that raised them and the generation before that. So the music grew, and the first sign that the establishment had succumbed, that they had thrown out the white flag, that they had surrendered, and gone with it, came also from music rather than something that had happened in society or some editorial. That was when the last vestige of conservative music in this country recorded a song called ''Kokomo'' with Perry Como using the basic R & R riff—Perry Como actually did a R&R song, and I think after that it signaled everybody that if you can't beat 'em, join 'em.

On an everyday basis, we don't realize how much we were affected by music, by what it says, what we read about what we hear; it affects us so slowly, but surely we evolve into a life-style we never would have thought of getting into because the effect of music is subliminal. If you hear a song you may run out and buy it, but you don't run out and change your clothes and change your hair and start taking drugs; I mean, this evolves—attitudes. Because everything comes from an attitude. I mean I see things that I initiated for years run down, and there's nothing I can say about it because I put it out there and I didn't stamp it—if it affected people I accomplished what I wanted to accomplish, it's the people's idea now; they will go ahead and say things they heard me say, and honestly believe it's their idea, because I didn't lecture them, I just let it hang out there. When people stop me and say, ''Man you had no idea how you affected my life!'' what can I say but ''Thank you very much.'' That's quite a compliment and I guess I did! Imagine if I did that, what the Beatles did all over the world!

It is true, of course, that by the late sixties the traditional ''boy-girl'' relationship in song had virtually disappeared. Actors in the new lyrics were singularly concerned with controlling their own destinies. As a consequence, romantic love was rejected as the exclusive requisite for engaging in a sexual relationship, and lyrics didn't describe people *falling* in love but actively *choosing* to do so. A sexually more casual generation than its predecessors dismissed chivalric amour in favor of the person free of ties or obligations. Yet it didn't take long for the Beatles to inquire, "All the lonely people, where do they all come from?" This was a musical generation in open rebellion against middle-class values, expressing what Lionel Trilling called "adversary culture"—a culture avidly opposed to prevailing norms of morality and cultural expectations. This music had come a long way from the early rock that was dedicated to the middle-class ideological strains of Tin Pan Alley. In fact, the messages were as different as those of Joseph McCarthy and Eugene McCarthy.

Rock in the mid-fifties was a paean to money and consumption. Chuck Berry's "car songs," "Mabellene," "No Money Down," and "You Can't Catch Me" emphasized speed, chrome-plated-shiny-bright-new engines, low down payments, and conspicuous consumption. The message was one of the girl's hair flying in the breeze while the radio blared "Rock Around the Clock." Even now I can close my eyes and remember a red Chevrolet convertible cruising Union Turnpike in Queens, New York, searching for girls while the radio played "Gee" by the Crows. With that car and "that" music I thought of myself as irresistible to nubile females who had recently discovered their own sexuality. Unhappily, my fantasy and reality rarely converged. Nonetheless, the possibility of success remained undiminished. This was the vision a car salesman relied on when he tried his hard sell on High School Harry. When asked why he sang about cars, Chuck Berry replied, "It's because everybody has one or dreams about one." He surely wasn't the critic of capitalist values and neither was his music.

MABELLENE
As I was motorvatin'
over the hill,
I saw Mabellene in a
Coupe de Ville.
Cadillac rollin' on the
open road,
Tryin' to outrun my V-8
Ford

In 1953 Clyde McPhatter and the Drifters recorded a song with the popular title "Money Honey." The words depict in semicomical blues the dilemma of romance without money. The protagonist, after a series of arguments with his landlord and "his woman," learns that the best things in life are not free; you need "money honey." In this sadly familiar situation, the reality principle intrudes on romance and wins. In three fairly repetitive verses, the subject is easily converted; he abandons his love, at least temporarily, for the pursuit of wealth. Victory for the Protestant Ethic! Like most black artists of the fifties, the Drifters were concerned with "dropping in" before they could consider "dropping out." "Money Honey" set the pattern for poor blues singers— white and black—of every generation. The pursuit of wealth transcended other values until affluence on an unprecedented scale was achieved in the sixties.

What I believe best illuminates this issue was the top hit of 1958, "Get a Job." Despite the fact that Charlie Gillett, author of *Sounds of the City*, refers to the Silhouettes as "revo-

lutionaries in disguise,'' their hit song (once one can deci-
pher the cacophony of "sha, da, das") offers a girl urging
her boyfriend to seek employment. Notwithstanding his inability to find a job and the bickering that ensues, he keeps
searching. On the one hand, the young man described in this
song is the potential "native son," a black filled with indig-
nation at his joblessness; but on the other, he is the prototypi-
cal example of the man striving for job, security, marriage,
and family. His anger about his joblessness and his striving
for the American dream are clear signs that he has accepted
normative behavior; his goals are not different from Chuck
Berry's, albeit he is more likely to be driving a V-8 Ford than
a Coupe de Ville.

> After breakfast every day,
> She throws the want ads
>   right my way,
> And never fails to say,
>   "Get a job."

In much the same way, conformity to the strictures of parental authority and social morality were espoused tacitly or
explicitly in many fifties "top ten hits." The Clovers' "One
Mint Julep" (1952) helped to set the tone for the decade
through a vivid description of alcohol's devastating effects.
A sense of impending damnation pervades the tune. But in
the last verse the black hero pulls himself out of alcoholism's
social pit and proclaims that he is through drinking. After all,
he paid a very high price for his fling—six unwanted children. To this very day, I still associate excessive drinking
with everlasting doom in Dante's Inferno, a fact that is easily
attributed to this song. Contrast this attitude with the alleged

joys obtained from the use of drugs that appear so frequently in lines from sixties songs.

> I don't want to bore you,
> with my trouble
> But from now on I'll be
> thinking double,
> I'm through with flirting
> and drinking whiskey—
> I got six extra children
> from getting frisky.

Johnny Cash also read the temper of the age properly by telling his audience to "Walk the Line" (1956). There is a redemptive quality to this tune's lyrics; they suggest that anyone can be saved if he has a true love who gives him the will to change and the guidance to maintain the "right" direction. In many respects this song was like a popular children's story of that era, *Tootle*. This little train was incorrigible; it insisted on riding off the tracks and onto the newly seeded grass. His mother was very angry. She scolded Tootle and said, "If you want to grow up to be a locomotive you'd better get back on the tracks like the rest of us." Tootle resisted at first, but he learned. And when he learned to ride on the tracks, he did indeed become a successful locomotive (Q.E.D.). In the 1970s children were offered *The Strange Story of a Frog Who Became a Prince,* the tale of a frog who does not want to be changed into the proverbial handsome prince—a message very different from its fairy-tale origins.

Typically Chuck Berry had the same conformist view. In "Almost Grown," even with its barely repressed anger, he depicts a guy who breaks no rules, romances and marries his girl, and ultimately settles down in his hometown. This character is a latter-day Jack Armstrong, a figure of primordial American mythology.

He is also the same character who in Berry's "School Days" studies dutifully in an effort to get good grades. In spite of many diversions, like "the guy behind you," who is more interested in fooling around than studying, he knows that if he keeps his nose to the grindstone there is plenty to look forward to at the juke joint. This is two and a half minutes of pure "Ozzie and Harriet."

Shadows of My Mind
Long Island Press, May 25, 1959

If Pat Boone or Elvis Presley get tough, Columbia's Herb London can always take them in the pivot. London, 6-foot 5-inch center on the Lion basketball team, has invaded the Boone-Presley field by recording two songs for Buzz Records and the Columbia junior is hopeful of a successful singing career. Boone, of course, is an honor graduate of Columbia's School of General Studies. Until this winter, London had no musical pretentions. He was entering his junior year in Columbia College, majoring in history with hopes for a teaching career. He had lettered in basketball as a reserve in 1957–58 and was looking forward to improving his status as biggest man on the varsity this season.

Then like a bolt from the blue (Light Blue, that is) came a series which led inexorably to an early-December recording date, March release of a record and who knows what in the future.

First the details: London's record was released early this week by Buzz Records. It is in juke boxes on and near the Columbia campus, and in Baltimore, Philadelphia, New Haven and Ansonia, Conn. It will be released next week in Washington, Albany and Schenectady. The songs are

"We're Not Going Steady," and "Hey Red." The former, a ballad, is considered the best bet for popularity.

"This is my first venture of this kind," the poised recently-turned-20 London remarks. "I always liked to sing and did while a counselor at Camp Oxford and in my fraternity (Sigma Alpha Mu). But I never did anything professionally.

"Then a friend of mine said I should try out for an agent he knew. The agent sent me to someone else and so on through several auditions. I finally wound up with a song-writer and the president of Buzz Records.

"They were impressed I guess, and the record date followed." There is a good story on that. Let's let London tell it.

"They set the record date for Dec. 8 or 9, I believe," London continues. "It was an afternoon session scheduled to last about 2½ hours. We had basketball practice that afternoon in preparation for our trip to Syracuse on Dec. 10, and the coach told me that if I was late for practice I could forget about the trip. We were preparing a special defense.

"I was a little worried. But it worked out fine. I made practice on time and made the trip."

Even when there is no pot of gold at the end of the rainbow and the job pumping gas is trying ("Too Much Monkey Business"), Berry sings "Johnny B. Goode." Berry may have been all passion and sizzling discontent, as some rock critics have suggested, but his lyrics are as irrepressibly conformist as the proverbial "organization man."

There was no social revolution in Berry's lyrics. Who else in the sixties could write "New York, Los Angeles, oh how I yearn for you" ("Back in the U.S.A.") The so-called generation gap of this decade passed him by. In "Sweet Little Sixteen" he told of a girl virtually begging her mother for permission to attend a rock show. It is interesting to compare this late-fifties reliance on parental authority with the view expressed by the Mamas and Papas in their hit song of six years later: "Go where you wanna go/Do what you wanna do." Of course very few people do what they want, but the expression of this liberationist goal revealed a shift in public attitudes or at the very least a shift in the attitudes of the average teenager in the sixties.

On the subject of respect for one's parents, Berry wasn't alone. Phil Spector wrote of his father: "To know is to love him." Eisenhower was America's paternal figure, and the pop music reflected a keen interest in and respect for prevailing norms. Ike didn't listen to rock as far as I can tell, but rock listened to him. When the Everly Brothers sang "Wake Up Little Suzie" they portrayed the embarrassment of having to face Suzie's parents after "oversleeping." The "trouble was deep" and the consequences palpably horrible. This seems and probably is light years away from Bob Dylan's "You can do anything that you want to baby."

What the contrast suggests most clearly is the change from an incipient revolution to one completely germinated.

Two writers who were early devotees of the "generation gap" (Jerry Leiber and Mike Stoller) tried to depict teenagers' conception of their parents in the very successful "Yakety Yak" (1957). The manifest form of this song is a series of continual, peremptory commands with the admonition "Don't talk back." What is curiously omitted from these lyrics is any mention of rebellion against arbitrary orders. For a generation suckled on fifties values, "Don't talk back" was a sufficient reminder that no explanation could satisfy Mom and Dad when they couldn't or wouldn't be persuaded. Although the song obviously intends chastisement of insensitive parents, it also seems to legitimize parental authority through the apparent acceptance of demands.

> Take out the papers and the
>   trash,
> Or you don't get no spending
>   cash;
> If you don't scrub that
>   kitchen floor,
> You ain't gonna rock 'n' roll
>   no more.
> Yakety yak, don't talk back

In their sequel to "Yakety Yak," Lieber and Stoller, in another song recorded by the Coasters, characterized the marginal man of the decade, "Charlie Brown." Charlie is the educational pariah; he is the class clown and village idiot. He is invariably abused ("Why is everybody always pickin' on me?"), yet he is often guilty of wrongdoing. He is a sad sack but a source of amusement to his peers. He could be Bob Dylan's lamentable character in "Subterranean Homesick Blues." But by the sixties the erstwhile buffoon had become a contemporary hero. As Dylan had explained, "The Times They Are A Changin'," with Charlie Brown in the vanguard. This vagabond of schoolyard humor emerged as the sixties hero—a combination of Abbie Hoffman and Benjamin.

> Charlie Brown, Charlie Brown
>   He's a clown, that Charlie Brown
> He's gonna get caught
>   Just you wait and see
> Why is everybody always
>   pickin' on me?

The one theme that has always been the focus of pop music is love. As a commodity, nothing has sold better. Virtually every couple in America looks back nostalgically to a song that symbolizes true love. The past is cleverly wrapped in a melody. Almost from the moment of birth, to one's first love, to a confirmation, engagement, and marriage, a song marks the occasion. Americans don't sing simply to feel good but to remember the past.

To this day, every time I hear "Sh-Boom" by the Chords, I'm reminded of a boyhood friend who decided that we could break the Guinness record for continuous renditions of a popular tune. We sang "Sh-Boom" more than one thousand consecutive times. I even asked Stanley where in the *Guinness Book of World Records* this achievement was recorded. I still consider this one of my more notable boyhood accomplishments.

Rock titles of the fifties portrayed the expectation and evolution of love for teenagers raised on Margaret O'Brien films, which had a simple inevitability. Love wasn't complicated, and neither was Margaret. When her heartstrings were tugged, wedding bells could be anticipated in three scenes. The same progression prevailed in the sounds of the fifties. Love's labors started with "Till Then," progressed to "Sixteen Candles," "Goodnight Sweetheart, Goodnight," and "Pledging My Love," then moved on to "Church Bells May Ring," "I Want You, I Need You, I Love You," "All I Have to Do Is Dream," and culminated with "I'm Gonna Get Married." The process was considered as inexorable as gravitation. For Frankie Lyman and the Teenagers, "Why Do Fools Fall In Love?" was as simple to answer as "Why do birds sing?" and "Does rain fall from up above?" Likewise, Sonny James sang of love with true devotion, and Jack Scott tunefully gave his version of "My True Love."

Fidelity, institutional stability, "love and marriage," courtship and exalted love were the values usually conveyed in fifties rock love songs. When "As Long As I Live" was recorded in the late fifties, it needed no explanation. For guys who stood in front of bowling alleys humming rock songs, God was in his heaven and all wasn't quite right with the world. But there wasn't anything a pizza and coke couldn't make somewhat better.

A decade later, we were told God is dead, and Dusty Springfield dramatized the change in values with the equally obvious "You Don't Have To Say You Love Me." While sex may have been implicit in early rock, by 1970 it was as explicit as the censors would allow. Murray The K may have prescribed watching submarine races at Plum Beach in the early sixties, but by the end of the decade the submarines had surfaced. Elvis Presley sang "Love Me Tender" in the fifties, but ten years later Neil Diamond was a "Solitary Man," Simon and Garfunkel had abandoned love completely by opting for total withdrawal ("I Am a Rock"), and Janis Joplin was screaming that love is bondage. Needless to say, marriage had also come to be seen as social bondage. Compared to most contemporary rock lyrics, those combined values of the fifties now seem as anachronistic as the proverbial horse and carriage.

If one ignores Marshal McLuhan—not a very easy thing to do—and concentrates on the message, not the medium, one might argue that there was very little radical about the ideas expressed in early rock music. Charles Reich contended that rock "is not a pastime but a necessity" for developing the "new consciousness." But, of course, rock was nourished in the age of McCarthyism. It was more an outgrowth of immanent revolution than imminent revolution. That rock was once a medium for imbibing bourgeois culture seems silly by contemporary standards, unless it is examined in historical perspective. Rock may have offended middle-class parents with its style, but for those who listened, the message was essentially a tribute to the status quo. Ten years later (in the mid-sixties) that fact was hard to remember and even harder to believe.

Shadows of My Mind
Time, July 23, 1956

The nation's elders fumed, fretted, legislated, and pontificated last week over the socking syncopations of "rock 'n' roll."

Items:

• After a riot in Asbury Park, N.J.'s Convention Hall that sent 25 vibrating teen-agers to the hospital, Mayor Roland J. Hines slapped a rock-'n'-roll ban on all city dance halls. Taking the hint, Jersey City cancelled Jazzman Paul Whiteman's "Rock 'n' Roll Under the Stars" show at the 24,000 seat Roosevelt Stadium. Cried anguished sponsor Ed Otto: "We were executed by remote control."

• Bandsman Bill (Rock Around the Clock) Haley, whose Comets were among the groups shut out by the Jersey City ban, put a defense of sorts on records in pounding choruses of a ditty called "Teenager's Mother," by referring to the Charleston of the twenties.

• In San Jose, Calif. rioting rock 'n' rollers routed 73 policemen, injured eleven people, did $3,000 worth of damage to a dance hall before they were evicted. Neighboring Santa Cruz banned rock 'n' rollers from civic buildings.

• In San Antonio rock 'n' roll was banned from city swimming-pool jukeboxes because, said the city council, its primitive beat attracted "undesirable elements" given to practicing their spastic gyrations in abbreviated bathing suits.

• Piano tuner O. J. Dodd told fellow delegates to the National Piano Tuners' convention in Kansas City that rock 'n' roll is raising hob with the nation's keyboards. For the first time in his long professional career, he said, he had seen a piano's thick bass chord snapped by a pianist flailing out a thundering rock 'n' roll chorus.

The major sociological comment of the week was that of Roosevelt University Sociologist Dr. S. Kirson Weinberg who saw in rock 'n' roll a manifestation of the insecurities of the age, added that "the effects of the music are more predominant in girls." Or perhaps it was that of the reader of the Denver Post who wrote: "This hooby doopy oop-shoop, ootie ootie boom boom de-addy boom, scoobledy goobledy dump—is trash."

In revolutionary terms, this second stage was an attempt to change social orthodoxy with an unorthodox style. The change was not intended to be substantive. The moderates who brought it about had no idea of the power they held in their guitars; their yellow brick road to ascendency was painted only with dollar signs.

But as in all revolutions these moderates—who built a foundation for change—ultimately gave way to the extremists: Chuck Berry ushered in James Brown; Elvis, the Beatles; The Big Bopper, Mick Jagger. Emotionally the rock moderates were trapped by the revolutionary process. As they bid to compete with the extremists, they were obliged to alter their style and consequently lost the audience that had made them popular in the first place. By definition these rock moderates were not monomaniacal about social change. That was incidental. Their lyrics were often silly and farcical. They believed teenagers would ultimately have to conform—this rock music was a fling, a juvenile fantasy. Rock moderates wanted common sense, comforts, and compromise, values deeply rooted in the nation and in their music. "This Land Is Your Land" is the title of a folk song the moderates imbibed. For them this was a fabulous land with prosperity and stability for all, conditions even their music couldn't disturb. But in the throes of revolution, when trends are not clear, the moderate is often myopic.

Ten years after Chuck Berry sang a tribute to this nation in "Back in the U.S.A." (1958), the conventional wisdom of the moderates seemed to be folly. Pandora's box had been opened, and the revolution was in full flower.

FOUR

A TYPOLOGY OF EARLY ROCK REVOLUTIONISTS

*T*he word *revolutionist* conjures up a cliche for the every-day citizen. Proustian nuances are not considered; a revolu-tionary is viewed as a seedy, unshaven beatnik, prone to vio-lence. There are, of course, the prosaically negative stereotypes in which the revolutionary is a failure, suffering from envy, who wishes to tear down the system because of an inferiority complex. And there is the positive stereotype in which this revolutionary is a working-class hero who reads Marx and Lenin before going to bed and displays all the charisma of Norman Mailer with his friends. Both of these interpretations are aimed at satisfying human senti-ments rather than describing objective reality.

On one point, however, there is consensus: the revolution-ist is a carrier, who wittingly or unwittingly transports the seeds of change. This figure becomes the embodiment of a new social order, sometimes by dint of personality, but most times because his supporters choose to see this person as a pure reflection of their wishes. By and large, the scenario of the revolutionary is very much like those who are led. The idea that the revolutionary will spring majestically from the ranks of the poor to lead some general social uprising is one of those myths that owes its origin to the fantasies of the radical chic bourgeoisie.

The revolutionist pretends that what is propounded is new, that the past is the enemy of this form of progress. Yet every culture derives its identity and character from its location in time. People cannot exist without memories; neither can societies. This is not to suggest that traditions are immutable. On the contrary, tradition is part of a pattern of persistence and change in which nothing stands still and nothing changes completely.

What distinguishes modern revolutionaries from their counterparts in the past is the belief that true humanity must be emancipated from every vestige of traditional boundaries. This explains, in part, the constant experimentation in rock music, as if the structure of music itself were limiting. This belief also accounts for the antiauthoritarian impetus of contemporary social thought so well described by Robert Nisbet in his essay on authoritarianism in our time. It explains why this generation invents and reinvents, with material as the age suggests, a "new era," "a last utopia," "the Age of Aquarius," *The Greening of America,* as if in each new order one might find one's soul in evangelical distinction between a "before" and an "after," or a "with it" and an "out of it."

In our time—this period from approximately 1953 to the present—a revolutionary has been a cultural figure who represents the will of a discontented subculture or is shrewd enough to know how to capture the spirit of discontentedness. This definition includes various permutations: the sincere, cynical, and neutral advocates of radical change. There are revolutionaries of genuine talent whom even conservatives see as worthy of respect. Their own achievement may have been limited by social or career barriers. Had it not been for the changing social climate, they would probably have lived in obscurity. It was the times coming together with unique talent that catapulted several figures into the spotlight. (Fats Domino is one such example, Chuck Berry another.)

Then there are the cynics who use the social climate for their own brand of revolution, usually a zealous assault on any and all tradition. This cultural figure is reminiscent of the Russian professor in G. K. Chesterton's "The Yellow Bird," a story that appears in *The Poet and the Lunatics*. In this tale Professor Ivanhov, obsessed with emancipation, conceives of ways to free living things from their "arbitrary" confines in nature. First, he liberates his canary from the cage, only to discover it has been torn limb from limb in the forest. Next he liberates his goldfish by smashing their bowl, only to find they die on the ground wriggling for a final breath. And finally he attempts to free his own soul from his body by blowing himself up. It is not so farfetched to see the analogy between this position and the finale of the group The Who: in an act of frenzy they destroy their instruments onstage in a moment that at once suggests liberation from musical structure and nihilism. Yet who among their fans has the wealth to engage in a similar act of destruction, and who in more sober moments expects this existential act to subvert musical boundaries?

Then there are the neutrals, those revolutionists who genuinely don't know what influence for change they have exerted. These are people with marginal talent and little vision, who, if truth be known, are the beleaguered leaders of a movement they do not understand and, if events had not thrust them in the limelight, would probably resist.

For the aficionado of rock it is comforting to believe that this music was composed by idealists aspiring for a better world. It is heartening to think that there are people who would put the dross of this world behind them for the purity of idealism, for noble aspiration. But this is not the way in which the rock revolution evolved. The distinguishing mark of this revolution is that it was made by average people whose lyrics raised expectations of high standards and "a new level of consciousness," but whose personal behavior was by and large strikingly mundane and distinctly self-indulgent. This, I should hastily add, is not a basis on which to evaluate musical accomplishments, as Albert Goldman does, by implication, in his book *Elvis*. It is, however, a necessary preliminary to understanding the relationship between the climate of opinion and the role of the artist—that amalgam of expectation and music that transforms musicians into alien characters whom they don't actually wish to personify.

Eric Hoffer in *The True Believer* makes the point that revolutions are made by "men of words," by so-called intellectuals. His argument is that the repressed intellectual whose talents have not impressed others will become the fanatical revolutionist. Marat was the neglected scientist; Robespierre the frustrated essayist; Lenin the inchoate philosopher; Mussolini the would-be scholar. Each in his way nurtured dreams of grandeur that turned into thwarted personal ambition and hatred against the society that didn't appreciate them.

The rock revolutionist, in contrast, is typically the ritual maker, the figure who brings people together. This is no thwarted intellectual, but rather a common person whose words are devoid of meaning even as they tap pleasant aspirations and have the sweetness of sounds easily recalled. The prototypes developed comprise common human beings united by the will to perform and to be successful, yet unknowingly inviting a revolution in values and sensibilities as stark as any in our history—a claim, I submit, that only future historians can support or refute.

Bobby Darin was what every midwesterner considered a New Yorker to be—brash, glib, slick, risk defying, and shameless. He didn't know how to take no for an answer. For Darin there were only one-way signs painted on the road to success. And he would cajole, lie, and charm you out of your boots to get on the fast lane. Darin wasn't an innovator; he wasn't one of those founding fathers of rock to whom the young pay ritualistic homage. But in his way he made rock acceptable to an audience that had formerly considered this music the private preserve of the young. In his way, Darin married rock and pop; he was best man at a wedding between WINS (the station that discovered rock) and WNEW (the station that adamantly held on to pop).

If he had a shred of humility, he probably would have been singing with Dion and the Belmonts. But in the late fifties nothing could keep this Italian Duddy Kravitz down except doubts about himself. He courted Murray The K knowing full well that Murray was at the top of his career and could make gold hits as he wished. He picked up the title "Splish Splash" from Murray's mother, wrote the song, and gave Murray part of the copyright. Murray made that song a smash hit in 1958, and Bobby emerged in the fast lane with all the lights synchronized in green.

Shadows of My Mind
Life, January 11, 1960

Though still short of his goal—"to establish myself as a legend by the time I'm 25"—Darin is moving in the right direction at a dead run. Summing up his progress to date, the impatient proprietor of King Kong Inc. says, "With *Mack* I have knocked down my biggest door. The public knows me." Recognition has also come from big league entertainers. His friend Sammy Davis, Jr., proudly dubs only *like* people a star, he says. "It's not open house here, not a party going on all the time. I don't have the entourage because I don't have the insecurity. Then," he adds, "of course, if nobody comes into my dressing room between shows, that bugs me too."

This was quite a step for a young man named Bob Cassotto whose father died before he was born and who survived by fighting his way from one end of the Bronx to the other using all the wiles in the bag of tricks street kids quickly learn. After recording "Queen of the Hop" in 1958, Bobby was at the top of the world—two hits in succession, a long-term Decca contract, and the recognition he craved. But Darin wanted to show audiences there was a secret Sinatra in his soul waiting to be set free. This creature of rock music weaned on doo-wop was eager to demonstrate he could *really* sing.

In 1959 he recorded "Dream Lover" and "Mack the Knife"—clearly a crossover to pop. Yet Darin preserved that special rock quality that gave these tunes distinction. When he sang "Dream Lover" in a cadence that borrowed from the roots of rock 'n' roll, the bridge was complete. Pop would never be the same—not for Tony Bennett, not for Frank Sinatra. Rock had won a victory, and Darin was leading the legions in an assault on the pop charts. His prize was a motion picture career launched with a marginal film called *Come September* and a marriage to Miss National Princess of the late fifties, Sandra Dee. Dee, who had the image of the blond, squeaky-clean, beautifully groomed, Waspy, middle American, was the dream girl Darin sang about and unquestionably coveted. Her image was everything Darin's wasn't, an image immortalized in the ''Sandra Dee'' song from *Grease:*

> Look at me, I'm Sandra Dee
> Lousy with virginity
> Won't go to bed till I'm legally wed,
> I can't, I'm Sandra Dee.

By the mid-sixties Darin's career was going against the rising tide of hard rock. His marriage was on the rocks, and his fame proved to be as ephemeral as last week's news. He tried to capture a new image by discarding his wig and singing antiwar songs, but audiences still wanted to hear ''Won't You Come Home, Bill Bailey?'' as only Darin could sing it.

In 1973 Darin died of a heart condition. He was thirty-seven years old, a rare talent whose major contribution to rock music was his effort at hybridization. Darin was one of the few rock singers who could cover Ray Charles without embarrassing himself. In my opinion he was the first white performer with soul. Here was a revolutionary with an accommodative spirit, a rock creation who transformed the soporific harmonies of traditional pop music into MOR (middle of the road) rock. It may not seem like much today, but in its time this transformation was a giant step in a cultural revolution.

If, as many cultural historians suggest, the 1950s was a period of quiescence and political consensus, this condition was not affirmed by the emerging musical sounds of the period. One of them was perhaps the most direct, lineal antecedent of Southern white music of the late forties and fifties, sometimes known as rockabilly. This convergence of hillbilly and blues was a marriage of convenience between familiar southern themes and style. The central concerns were unrequited love, whiskey consumption, and melancholy about growing old too soon; the style drew on the slurred, sexy, modulated Southern pattern of speech that seems like a combination of put-on and put-down. There were many who mastered this music, from Mr. "Blue Suede Shoes," Carl Perkins, to Jerry Lee Lewis, Roy Orbison, Buddy Holly, and of course Elvis Presley. But the one who best exemplified the simplicity and inherent sexuality of this music and its conflict with prevailing social norms was Gene Vincent.

Vincent's music was derivative, like that of most of his contemporaries. He began singing in a Norfolk, Virginia, church and never lost sight of his musical tradition. Yet his music was intentionally sexy, of dubious taste, and a melange of contradictions strung together, I suspect, almost at random. After injuring his leg during a navy stint in Korea, Vincent walked with a limp the rest of his life. Upon returning to Virginia he formed a group called the Blue Caps named after Eisenhower's golf cap. The members wore copies of the cap but Vincent never doffed his. In 1956 he sang "Be-Bop-a-Lula" (written by his buddy, Sheriff Tex Davis) in a Los Angeles talent contest and won first prize. The song went on to become a platinum seller and launched Vincent's career. What most of his fans didn't know was that the song was inspired by the Little Lulu comic character but concerned a Lulu who wasn't diffident and was something more to her boyfriend than the butt of his jokes.

She's the girl in the red, blue jeans,
She's the queen of all the teens.
She's the one that I know.
She's the one that loves me so.

By 1957 there was no subtlety in his music. Vincent was in the vanguard of bad taste. His recording of "I'm Lookin' for a Woman with a One Track Mind" was so heavily affected by an echo chamber that every "a-huggin and a-fuggin" left nothing to the listener's imagination. He sang "Lotta Lovin'," a modest success, with the sexy incantation continually repeated, "Well, I wanna, wanna want a lot of lovin'/ Well, I wanna, wanna want a lot of huggin'/Oh baby don't forget I'm goin' to you yet/I want you lovin' uh huh you bet."

By 1960 Vincent's career was in eclipse. He left for England hoping to recapture his success of the mid-fifties. But it didn't happen. He suffered from depression and bleeding ulcers, which ultimately resulted in his death before his thirty-seventh birthday.

Shadows of My Mind
"Gene Vincent Dead at 36," *Rolling Stone,*
November 11, 1971

On stage, limping around in leather, all grease and sinister sensuality, with a vocal style not unlike Presley's, Vincent established himself as a solid attraction around the world. He spent his last few years working mostly in England, where despite steadily declining popularity, he was still in demand in small pubs on the outskirts of London or in workingman's clubs in the North. Britain's old Teddy Boys and Greasers, some of whom still affect drape jackets and ducktail haircuts, would continue to revere Vincent as a legend. . . .

Vincent was both literally and figuratively a classic rocker. His music inspired young British groups like the Sex Pistols, whose aesthetic revolt was a latter-day version of Vincent's assault on sexual mores. Gene Vincent wasn't a prodigious musical talent. His material grew out of poor, white, Southern surroundings and flared briefly with a constituency that wished "to taste forbidden fruit" on phonograph records. Vincent served it up—concealed at first, and then overtly, in defiance of everything in his background. His revolutionary status came, not from his notoriety, but from his use of rock music as a challenge to middle-class sensibilities.

If there was one early explorer who dug so deeply into the rock vein that others could follow and profit beyond their wildest dreams, it was Little Richard. Here was the man who gave rock its funky, unique, unorthodox style. Little Richard, born Richard Penniman, gave the music a starburst of moans, sighs, screams, and panting that made rock singing as different from other vocals as ice cream is different from ice. His voice wasn't heard; it was experienced.

Richard was the third of fourteen children. At thirteen he was thrown out of the house and went to live with a white couple who owned a nightclub in Macon, Georgia, his hometown. Little Richard learned how to perform in that club. Within a year he learned how to turn on a crowd with his gospel, jive—any sound alive. By sixteen he had a record contract at R.C.A., but his early records were rather pedestrian rhythm and blues with none of the spontaneity and zaniness of his later works.

In 1955 Richard recorded an obscene ditty he often sang in the streets. It was sanitized for the record, but it still had the effect of acid hitting flesh. All of the vocal inhibitions were removed; Little Richard, with blaring voice and a hard-charging saxophone behind him, sang "A Girl Named Daisy." He had found his persona. He was pure sexual excitement; his agent called him "the handsomest man in rock 'n' roll." That, of course, wasn't all. He built bridges across decades to other rock performers: The Beatles, the Rolling Stones, Creedence Clearwater Revival owe hits to Little Richard. Other performers such as Screamin' Jay Hawkins tried to emulate Richard's howl, and with "I'll Put a Spell on You" Hawkins almost succeeded. But Richard was there first.

From the mid-fifties through the early sixties, Little Richard was a cottage industry. He took Specialty Records to the top of the charts with "Long Tall Sally," "Slippin' and Slidin'," "Rip It Up," "Ready Teddy," "The Girl Can't Help It," "Lucille," "Send Me Some Lovin'," "Keep A'knockin'," and "Good Golly Miss Molly," to name a few. The songs were based on kinetic drive, which Little Richard had in abundance, and childlike foolishness, which elicited peculiar sounds to startle and awaken dreamy, lovesick adolescents.

By the sixties Richard had turned from rock to God. He studied prophecy and sang evangelical songs. One of them, "He Got What He Wanted (But He Lost What He Had)" contains a marvelously ironic insight into Little Richard's conversion with its cost and reward. His later attempts at rock records failed badly, partly because he had become a caricature of himself. His wildness was out of control, and his records were without ballast. In the late seventies he admitted to being a homosexual with a drug problem.

Shadows of My Mind
Melody Maker, November 18, 1967

"I'm the greatest," shouted Little Richard. And in case we

didn't get the resemblance: "Don't you think I look like Cassius Clay or he looks like me? I was first."

Yet this is not the Little Richard whose frantic style shocked and seduced racially mixed audiences across the nation. Little Richard was many whites' first introduction to being on the wild side. His lyrics were puerile, a gallimaufry of sounds and grunts that could be reproduced by toddlers. But his presence, his energy, his unconventional music, his six inches of hair combed straight up in the front, his pencil-thin mustache—all conspired to make him the Rasputin of rock, a man who could hold listeners spellbound, even when his words had no meaning at all.

Fats Domino possessed none of the flash and passion of Little Richard; in fact, by comparison his music is like a lazy day under the magnolia tree. But Fats is the one revolutionist who maintains an organic tie to the past. He carries in his piano sounds the history of New Orleans jazz. Unlike the other revolutionaries I've mentioned, who share Nietzsche's claim that "only that which has no history is definable," Fats breathes New Orleans funeral marches and the memory of a boogie-woogie piano beat.

Fats was one of nine children. His father, a violinist, and his brother-in-law, Harrison Verrett, twenty years his senior, taught Fats how to play the piano. He took to the instrument like grits to ham. He circulated through all the clubs in New Orleans imbibing eight-bar riffs from the masters (Salvador Doucette, Huey Smith, Clarence "Frogman" Henry, Professor Longhair) and playing them back in his own unique style. In 1949 Dave Bartholomew and Fats wrote a song that permanently changed his name from Antoine Domino to Fats Domino. It was called the "Fat Man," and it was the first of dozens of hit records on the Imperial label and the beginning of a writing collaboration with Bartholomew that went on for twenty years.

For Fats the color line was not a fiction wrought by the media industry; it was a real barrier. His records were forced into the Procrustean bed of race music and, while they didn't languish, they didn't exactly set the world on fire either. In 1955 that situation changed with his first crossover success, "Ain't That a Shame," a song made even more popular by Pat Boone's "cover." There was a simplicity and charm in Fats's music. He had none of the raw power and sexuality of Little Richard. His style was one of good humor, ease, grace, and humility. That, as much as his music, accounted for his unprecedented appeal in the fifties.

One hit followed another as inexorably as gravity. "I'm in Love Again" was followed by "Blueberry Hill," "Blue Monday," "I'm Walkin'," "Whole Lotta Lovin'," "Be My Guest," "My Girl Josephine," "Don't Come Knockin' " and too many others to mention here. The ideas for his music came from the streets of New Orleans—expressions he heard, piano sounds in local bars, and the jazz strains that weave their way in and out of that city's history. In 1956 Fats recorded his biggest hit, "Blueberry Hill," a song he had wanted to record ever since he first heard Louis Armstrong's version of it many years before. None of his hits ever reached the top of the charts—even "Blueberry Hill" didn't make it—but in his time the Domino formula was like combining peaches and cream and a little spice. The result was predictable: instant success. If Fats sang "Put Your Arms around Me Honey" or "Jambalaya"—as he did—you could hear two notes and know he was singing, even if the songs had been recorded by hundreds of other performers.

Shadows of My Mind
Melody Maker, March 8, 1958

Rhythm and blues will last forever—Fats Domino.

It seems incongruous to call this Fat Man a revolutionist. After all, he represents a tradition that goes back to the turn of the century. But what Domino did was take rhythm and blues out of the closet and repackage it with a giant diamond ring, a broad smile, two hundred pounds of corpulence, and a buglelike falsetto voice that is one of a kind. This music, which was ostensibly for black audiences to dance to, was made palatable for whites by Domino's casual style and easy manner. His lyrics were not biting; there was never any serious intent to them.

He singlehandedly created the impression—a false impression, I might add—that the music was benign. Domino was a precursor for revolutionists who were biding their time. If one looked over his shoulder, what would one see? A band of angels from New Orleans, singing of sweetness and light, ingenuous good times, and simple emotions when one shed tears over a heartbreaking romance and found love on ''Blueberry Hill.'' Is there no coincidence between Richie's admiration for ''Blueberry Hill'' on ''Happy Days'' and the television program's obsessive recreation of a simpler, carefree and innocent era in the fifties? That was Fats Domino time. When dominos are lined up together, they make a wonderful make-believe barrier. But when one falls, they all fall. By the late sixties, Domino's popularity had significantly declined. He still performs, but it is ''memory lane'' material, not anything that will make the top forty.

In theories of revolution, it is part of the conventional wisdom to believe that, as the revolutionary message becomes extreme, popular support is dissipated even as power is concentrated. In the rock revolution the early leaders were common people who sought a broad base of support. They were emotionally moderate: they wished to titillate without tearing down a century of behavioral norms. Whether any visionary could have seen this early effort as the first stage in a dramatic epoch is almost beside the point. Once the first period of revolution is over, the struggle between moderates and extremists inevitably must arise. One may anticipate this conflict, but to circumvent it may be impossible, as the recent revolution in Iran indicates.

Extremists face combatants who must protect a status quo they were involved in creating—even if that status quo is newly formed around the unconventional sounds of a Little Richard and a Fats Domino. Once the wheel is turning, it tends to stay in motion. New musical innovations very quickly become the sounds of the past. It is only when the turning stops that one can look back and give credit where credit is due—or blame, as the case may be. "Top forty" radio shows have a way of digging graves for hits of only a few years ago. They become "blasts from the past" or "oldies but goodies" that are less than ten years old.

The early revolutionists loved their music, but they were unselfconscious about a social role. They didn't hate their times or intentionally promote social upheaval. They only wanted fun, rebellion within limits, moderate change, compromise. In a revolutionary period, we look back at those times nostalgically.

FIVE

ACCESSION—1957-1963

*I*n the first period of the rock revolution, from 1957 to 1963, the music world was swept by a wave of change that paralleled the change in social and political culture nationally. If Eisenhower in 1952 and again in 1956 represented stability in politics, Perry Como was the voice of stability in music. By the time Kennedy appealed to the nation for an expression of national idealism—a new frontier, which in a symbolic sense meant breaking new ground—Elvis Presley had already captivated youthful audiences with "All Shook Up" (1957). The hyperbole of political rhetoric and the revolutionary ethos of rock music met at the junction of youthful passions.

There was rampant in the land a fever with no known cure. It manifested itself in a national observance of "twisting," "stomping," and "bopping." As the rhetoric for change became more strident than in the early fifties, rock music adapted to the times.

The manifestations of teenage dissatisfaction have always appeared, in a variety of forms but with three persistent characteristics: rebellion, withdrawal, and escape. These three became the focus of a rock music sensitive to the currents of a new decade, the sixties. Culturally, this decade was highly significant. Perhaps it will be considered one of those "turning points in history." A chapter was proclaimed at an end, and the beginning of another era announced with all the pomp of a Hollywood opening. Idealism was at an apogee, due to the demographic fact that the baby boom generation was entering its teens. Rock became a national anthem.

When Gene Pitney wrote and the Crystals sang "He's a Rebel" (1952), the music and lyrics confirmed what demographic trends and political hyperbole had already suggested—teenage rebellion, which had formerly been treated as part of the ebb and flow of life, was now a national preoccupation.

> He's a Rebel and he'll never ever
>   be any good,
> He's a Rebel 'cause he never ever
>   does what he should,
> Well just because he doesn't do what
>   everybody else does,
> That's no reason why I can't give him
>   all my love.

A teenager who was not a James Dean fell into one of two other stereotypes that social thinkers had constructed and rock music well expressed: the escapist and the dreamer. The former description was well portrayed by Paul Anka's "Lonely Boy" (1959) and Del Shannon's "Runaway" (1961) and perhaps best described in "Teen Angel," recorded by Mark Dinning in 1960:

That fateful night the car was stalled
up on the railroad track
I pulled you out and we were safe
but you went running back.
What was it you were looking for
that took your life that night?
They said they found my high school
ring clutched in your fingers tight. . . .

The stereotype of the dreamer goes back to the 1956 Platters' hit "My Prayer," but I believe it is best represented by the Everly Brothers in "All I Have to Do Is Dream" (1958).

When I want you in my arms,
When I want you and all your charms
Whenever I want you all I have to do is dream,
Dream, dream, dream.

This period in which teenage concerns comprised the lyrics in rock songs was a cocoon stage—a period before the butterfly emerged. It was a period at the end of gestation, a time in which almost everyone knew a cultural revolution would be born, even though no one could be precise about its birthday.

As is always the case before the onset of something new in the arts, there was an obsession with form. If the fifties were a period of silence—exemplified by Samuel Beckett's preoccupation with "waiting" or John Cage's "aesthetic coda"— and the sixties were obsessed with noise of the "yeh! yeh! yeh!" variety, the era in between was one of rumbling. The rumbling suggested not only the coming storm but the degeneration of tradition and stability. Popular music of this time foreshadowed the change: its subtle challenge to innocence, norms, and conventional morality hinted at what was to come. It voiced the birth of a struggle between what is novel and what is lasting, the cultists of the new and the defenders of what we have.

The rock concert and the parallel folk concert of this era had all the trappings of teenage revival meetings; the former was for Holy Rollers, the latter for Unitarians who preferred a cerebral approach to celebration. But this was an exercise in twentieth-century antinomianism. Teenagers were set free from parental moral confinements through the dispensation of grace proclaimed in the gospel of either folk guitars or rock rhythms.

This was an interregnum, a time between rule without leadership and the true assumption of power. There was still an ingenuous quality to the music, illustrated, for example, by the controversy over that new dance, the twist. Critics decried it as lewd and uncreative. Geoffrey Holder said it was "a gimmick turned into a dance." Defenders said it was fun, free, interpretive, and natural. It was a tempest in a teapot, since the dance had a three-year life span. But the controversy ultimately demonstrated another stylistic concession rock obtained from an unwary public ordinarily critical of the music. In 1960 three hundred socialites paid $100 each to twist for eight hours with the dance's originator, Hank Ballard and his Midnighters, as ex–Atlanta mayor William Hartsfield boasted proudly that Ballard, a hometown boy, had launched the dance in Georgia in 1958. Chubby Checker covered the Ballard song in 1959, shamelessly calling himself Mr. Twist and tirelessly promoting the craze. It was a bonanza for him. He sold shirts, blouses, pants, socks, sweaters, scarves, towels, bracelets, rings, cuff links, record holders, and toys using the Chubby Checker name. His moniker promoted spaghetti and frankfurters and Twist instructions for television in the United States, Canada, Australia, and England. His royalties, income from the film *Twist Around the Clock,* and a fee of $2,500 a performance netted him more than a million dollars over a six-month period in 1961.

The twist was a twister in a literal sense: it moved large barriers out of the way and encouraged the belief that this fad would pass like all other adolescent fads. After all, how could a generation that sang "A-Tisket A-Tasket," "Three Little Fishes" and "Mairzy Doats" be critical of "Let's Twist Again"? As the editors of *Changing Times* (February, 1959) pointed out: "You restrain yourself from putting on the Irate Parent act. . . . Who wants to be a square in his own family circle? Instead, you go away smoldering, wondering how you can possibly make the kids understand what you find so unacceptable about the music they enjoy." Twenty years later this parental uneasiness and inability to understand were described by Pink Floyd as "Another Brick in the Wall."

This was also the era of manufactured teen idols. If you were smart and could get a Philadelphia office and a Bandstand imprimatur, you had an excellent chance of selling your product. Bob Marcucci was one of the supersalesmen who took this route. He found an attractive little Italian street kid from Philadelphia named Frankie Avalon, wrapped him in an image of the huggable, cute boy next door, and sold him to Chancellor records. Songs were carefully selected so as not to tax Avalon's limited singing range and to enhance his preteen appeal. At one record session, Marcucci suggested that Avalon pinch his nose to get a more nasal effect. What this gimmick did was to give Avalon his first hit, "Dede Dinah," and his trademark.

Marcucci also discovered another Philadelphia teenager at Southern High School who had the looks that spelled stardom: Fabiano Forte. His name was changed to Fabian; and his looks were described as a cross between Elvis and Ricky Nelson. What couldn't be changed was a voice that resembled that of a muffled chimpanzee. Fabian was the first to admit he couldn't sing. But Marcucci wasn't selling a voice—he was promoting sex appeal. Fabian was hyped as the Tiger Man, feline and ferocious. His songs (if you can call them that)—"Turn Me Loose," "Tiger," "Come On and Get Me"—were designed to stroke female fantasies rather than aesthetic sensibilities. In the teen idol business, Fabian was a hit.

It is interesting to compare these teen idols of the early sixties, whose appeal was based on somewhat innocent fantasies (e.g., "Venus," "Bobby Sox to Stockings," "Don't Throw Away All Those Teardrops") with Shaun Cassidy's music in the seventies. Cassidy, a product of television hyperbole, was the Avalon for a three-year period. However, there was a difference. Cassidy opened his act by standing behind a large screen so that only his silhouette was visible. As the music reached a crescendo and as he shook his rear furiously, he plunged through the screen singing, "Caroline Is Coming." This symbolism could not have been entirely lost on the female audience, age twelve and younger, who threw themselves into paroxysms of excitement, a demonstration of vicarious sexuality that made almost every parent embarrassed or uneasy. The contrast between Avalon and Cassidy provides a vivid portrayal of the moderate and the extremist separated by time and emotional deportment. One believed that the fabric of society could hold, with modest adjustments; the other was ready to unleash a tidal wave of emotion for a new social order. It may seem absurd to compare Avalon and Cassidy with political figures of a revolution. But as symbols, they do reflect a significant change in attitude that may be as startling as the political upheavals in 1917 and 1789.

The real schism in the music of this period was the emotional distance between the folk artists and rock musicians. In retrospect this may not seem like much of a controversy. But it once generated a lot of heat. The folk artists like Peter, Paul and Mary, Harry Belafonte and the Kingston Trio were like Mensheviks; eager for change, sensing what was in the air, they were nevertheless tied to traditions of the past.

Shadows of My Mind
Melody Maker, April 11, 1964

Mary Travers of Peter, Paul and Mary:
   What we try to do is to present the original meaning of the song. But to do it as it was done in the original is to be reporters. We're interpreters, and it's a case of being ourselves.

Folk music can hardly point to the future, since it is cultivated in history's soil. The immanent rock music of the Coasters, Little Richard, and Frankie Lyman was the Bolshevism of the period; irreverent and stirring, it proclaimed its autonomy from the past in style if not in substance.

While the musicians themselves now contend there was nothing to the dispute, those of us who reached adolescence during this period can't forget it. Murray The K told me that he was literally forced to close a rock show in Detroit because he had Peter, Paul, and Mary on the program. For rockers there could be no compromise; the reverse was also true for folk fans, of course. I can remember being castigated by my peers at Jamaica High School for preferring the Coasters to Harry Belafonte. My preference was described as mindless, tasteless, childish, and worse. I couldn't be deterred, but I do recall that Carol Fineburg wouldn't go to a party with me unless I recanted. Having to choose between Carol and the Coasters was easy; there were a lot of other girls to take to that party.

Yet this split in musical taste has a strangely recondite quality. Both groups were in opposition to the old order. It was on matters of impressions and constituencies that differences arose. Folk devotees considered themselves cerebral; while the artists sang of the masses, they sang to the bourgeoisie. Rock, on the other hand, was the music of the streets; it was unabashedly an example of mass cult, and its appeal in middle-class homes was reserved to those where the parents were overly permissive or desperately trying to win their children's affection. These musical forms, however, were united in challenging the high estimation of the moral and aesthetic value of traditional music.

Folk artists were indeed children of the Enlightenment. Like Pelagians who believe we are born innocent and pure, Pete Seeger and the Weavers were eternal optimists, singing about decent people and corrupt institutions. I always wondered who made those institutions corrupt, but that was beside the point. These were the flower children of the fifties exalting the working people as heroes and politicking from the refuge of their entertainment world for radical-liberal ideas consistent with their belief in a worldly utopia.

It was to this genre that artists like Judy Collins, Joan Baez, the Kingston Trio, the Limeliters, the Chad Mitchell Trio, the Brothers Four, the New Christy Minstrels, Peter,

Paul and Mary, and, of course, Bob Dylan gravitated. They wished to be commercial successes, but more than anything else they wanted to be true to their beliefs. There were compromises. How can one attack crass commercialism using the tools of commercialism? Youthful innocence suffered under the yoke of unyielding hypocrisy. It was one thing to ask rhetorical questions about warfare in "Blowin' in the Wind" and quite another to reduce the competition between artists that fosters success.

In the end, folk music couldn't sustain its purity. It was like the Candide of the twentieth century asking naive and interesting questions that cannot be answered. When Dylan picked up an electric guitar, folk music died as an influential musical form. In fact, Dylan said about rock, "In that music is the only true, valid death you can feel today off a record player." Was he referring to the rock-inspired death of folk?

As a memory, folk is the musical counterpart of religious saintliness. Its lyrics are not contaminated by moral dilemmas. It represents an impatience with life's complexities; it believes in a world of absolutes in which good and bad are easy to discern. While folk artists sang of human decency, their commitment was to moral absolutism. They saw violence as evil, capitalists as greedy, and "getting ahead" as a mirage. Their litany was based on "the people" writ large. This was romantic nationalism of the eighteenth century transposed to the twentieth. One could sing of "the infallibility of the people" (le peuple), as if the words themselves made the concept real. What was supposedly invoked was some forgotten inner unity that, when reawakened, gave audiences a sense of solidarity. But toward those who did not share its values, folk could be exclusive and "democratically" elitist. Its holier-than-thou approach to music may have heightened the moral sensibilities of some, but it exacerbated controversy with the rockers.

The authentic style of folk did ingratiate the music with college audiences, who assumed that folk was "real," a true expression of the people, as opposed to Tin Pan Alley pabulum. They listened to the words. (They were also the last generation to listen *only* to the words.) Folk *was* revolutionary in its content, but it omitted the significant feature of this rock revolution: the experience of uninhibited movement. It is movement, literally and figuratively, on which revolutions depend, and it was a lack of movement that ultimately vitiated folk music.

If folk in its archetypal form was at an end, Dylan built a bridge to all music with his "Bringing It All Back Home" and "Blonde on Blonde" albums in 1965 and 1966. Now the minstrel of the Enlightenment became the poet of Revolution. With "The Times They Are a-Changin' " and "Ballad of a Thin Man," the cycle was complete. Reflection was replaced by action, and the man of contemplation now argued, "Don't Think Twice, It's All Right," a song about love or, more accurately, about breakup, that revealed Dylan's social resentment. Surely Dylan didn't need to know which way the wind was blowing: he was a one-man hurricane who shed his mask of the contemplative Rousseau rooted in folk tradition to become the Robespierre of "It's All Over Now, Baby Blue." Here was the revolutionary who had given up his acoustic guitar for an electric one—a change that not only made Dylan rock but that married the style of folk protest to the iconoclasm of rock action.

In 1963 Skeeter Davis sang a song that went to number two on the charts, "The End of the World." This ballad represented the end of an era in music, a fear of apocalypse based on the Cuban missile crisis, and the specter of something new in the air. (That same year, Dylan wrote "A Hard Rain's A Gonna Fall," in which he described his own fear of nuclear war. "I'm a-goin' back out 'fore the rain starts a-fallin'./I'll walk to the depths of the deepest black forest.")

Also in 1963 there was a wind from the west, a musical sound that was refreshingly new, very much California, and based on the surfing craze—surf music. Surfers and their disciples, all bronzed beach lovers, spent their days on or near salt water, speaking and singing with the beat of the surf and in their own idiosyncratic argot. A "beach dolly," for example, was an "older" woman—about seventeen—whose "hodaddy" was a hot-rodder with sideburns and long hair. He might even have been a "hot-dogger"—an acrobatic performer on the surfboard.

Surfing was probably the first sport to emerge with its own music. It has been called everything from "wet rock 'n' roll" to "real beach music." And, although there were many surf music groups—e.g., Dick Dale, Surfaris, Chantays, the Dartells, and the Astronauts—one group represented this music best and took it to the top of the national charts—the Beach Boys and "Surfin' U.S.A."

What the Beach Boys sold to America was the California life of freedom, convertible cars, sun-tanned bodies, flaxen hair, having a "good" time, and waving goodbye to responsibility. Here were synthetic values served up in California red, white, and blue, masquerading as the national goal. And the music sold. In fact, its success was based partly on a craving for irresponsibility at a time when nuclear Armageddon didn't seem far off. In part, too, the emergence of surf music reflected a southern-tier life-style that claimed to be "mellow" and removed from the "rat race." Although to my knowledge he wasn't a surfer, Kookie Ed Byrnes, a relatively minor character on the 1958–62 television program "77 Sunset Strip," became a national celebrity for the same reasons. Kookie, a parking-lot attendant on the program, was "cool" in a very California way, swaggering, posturing, and forever combing his hair. With Connie Stevens, he recorded "Kookie Kookie, Lend Me Your Comb," a song in which Byrnes, using his own unique brand of jivey jargon, seemed to capture the new Western spirit.

What is important to realize about this music is in a sense what is important to understand about Sun Belt culture. This is a culture of affluence; children of divorce; existential values; instant gratification; fast cars traveling over great distances; wide-open spaces; rootlessness; new "highs"; and freedom on a scale never envisioned by our forefathers. Surfing is a perfect symbol for this ethos. It is dangerous and exhilarating; it is done alone; it pits man against nature in the best Western tradition. The surfer who hits the wave right thrills to unimaginable speed; but hit it wrong, and you "wipe out." In other words, while talent is required, the luck of the wave is definitive, and every wave is different, each surf unique. Here is existentialism American style. Talent, luck, and confronting a new situation each and every time are its components.

Shadows of My Mind
Melody Maker, August 22, 1964

Brian Wilson of the Beach Boys:
With us it wasn't a conscious thing to deliberately build a

music around surfing. It was just a lucky guess on my part to write lyrics that surfers would understand, to music they would like and dance to. We just want to be identified with the interests of young kids. That's why we also got into the hot rod scene. You know how kids love to talk about cars. What's more natural than to give them music to go with it?

Surf music is free of sophistication; it is natural in the way in which an adolescent might use that word. *Rough* might be an appropriate substitute. As Paul Gardner reported in the *New York Times,* August 10, 1963, "When the music gets too good, it isn't considered the real thing." The musical revolution rode this wave to its crest, building the ingenuous sounds of surfing to the high plateau of "Good Vibrations" by the Beach Boys, a song of such power and musical insight that its appearance must be seen as a benchmark moment in the history of rock. It is instructive that "My Son, the Surf Nut" could give way to "Vibrations." For what had happened was not only the development of taste and musical appreciation, but an inner turmoil—as vibrations symbolize—eager for expression. The song was like a contemporary fugue searching for exposition. At once playful and volatile, it gave its listeners a sense that rock music was pregnant with possibilities.

As is the case with all revolutions, there was a gap between deeds and declarations—between what these revolutionists were, what they would like to have been, and what they thought they were. Such gaps tend to occur when the absolutist spirit is widespread, when there is no truck with relative ideas, when there is reference only to Mankind, not to man.

However, during this period when clouds were filled with "hard rain" but were not yet open, the rock artist didn't quite fit this pattern of absolutism. The rocker represented escapism, good times, freedom—a form of cultural anarchism that rejects convention and unwittingly invites extremism. But the extreme had not yet arrived. As Ortega y Gasset noted, "To create a concept is to leave reality behind." What occurred during this time was a conceptualization of a new social order. The real world, meanwhile, seemed without direction.

What was occurring in music was like a stage in Darwinian evolution: only those that adapted, survived. In all revolutions there is a period before the full impact of change is felt. These are the years when moderates of a liberal stripe appear to be in control. It is the time of Mirabeau before Robespierre, Kerensky before Lenin, Barzagan before Khomeini, and the Beach Boys before the Beatles. Yet as the years pass, the forces of change conjoin to bring about its full impact. This is the moment when all dissenters have been deposed; when it is clear a new position has been realized.

For those who opposed the extremism in rock that gained ascendancy, the years before the Beatles seemed like halcyon days, a time for fun, fun, fun. Here was dissent without the self-engrossed preoccupation with authenticity. What later became an introspective quest for realization was now little more than having a good time. It would sound pretentious to label this period *fin de siecle,* but in a sense it was both the autumn of one era and the spring of a forthcoming season.

SIX

GERMINAL—1964

*I*n their determination to uproot everything of the *ancien regime,* the French revolutionists revised the calendar. They named twelve new months after the much-revered works of nature. Germinal was the month of buds, the time when the signs of birth are apparent. The inevitable flow of nature, with its time for rejuvenation and somnolence, was a perfect justification for the rigid determinists who believed that they too were instruments of the inevitable; in fact they envisioned themselves as the means through which the inevitable realized itself. They could not accept resistance to their proselytizing; the rejection of unbelievers was also seen as part of the inevitable flow of history by these visionaries who arrogated to themselves a special wisdom about the unknown future.

Pumped up with a messianic fervor about their place in history, revolutionists must spread the gospel of change that has been revealed to them. It is their ''destiny'' to do so. The Jacobins announced that they would transport the blessings of freedom around the globe; the Bolsheviks viewed themselves as the apostles of worldwide revolution.

In all cases revolutionists are intolerant, a function of their conviction that they are absolutely right. Theirs is the one truth of nature. To entertain other opinions is to invite error, sin, and doubt. In other words, tolerance itself is unforgivable. What they seek is a heaven on earth, the defeat of evil once and for all. Those who don't accept this view—the agnostics—become the victims of the revolution. For it is believed that, in order to get from where we are to where we'd like to be, a price must be paid in dislocation and human suffering. This is the faith of true believers who will do whatever it takes to impose their brand of virtue on the rest of mankind.

The germinal year of the rock revolution was 1964. An obscure English rock group from Liverpool gave the British revenge for their defeat in the American Revolution. The Beatles had launched the British invasion of America, and our musical scene would never be the same again. In 1964 their five single records occupied the top five positions on the trade charts. "I Wanna Hold Your Hand" was the top seller of the year, and youths were now infected with something called "Beatlemania," a combination of hysteria, lovesickness, and exaltation.

Shadows of My Mind
Life, August 28, 1964

Local promoters are under contract to hire a special force of at least 100 cops to guard the Loved Ones in every city, and police officials worry that 100 might not be enough. Hotels in San Francisco and Los Angeles panicked and evicted the Beatles before they arrived. Los Angeles' Lockheed Airport was so concerned lest teenagers run out onto the runway that it forbade any plane bearing Beatles to land there. So desperate is the crisis that latest plans call for a chartered plane to fly the Beatles in the dead of night, like a troop movement in wartime or a shipment of gold to Fort Knox.

This was the year of the Beatle. Yet their music was sanitized rock 'n' roll, a rip-off of Little Richard, Chucky Berry, and Elvis. It was probably fair to say, as the *New York Times* of that year did, that the Beatles were "one-tenth hair, one-tenth music and eight-tenths publicity." They were nurtured on Bill Haley, Elvis impersonators like Tommy Steele and Cliff Richard, and Chuck Berry. But their unique style had not yet evolved. In fact, it could be argued that in the late fifties, when their name changed from the Quarrymen to the Silver Beatles, they had no style at all. Lillian Roxon, rock authority, wrote, "Musically, they were fairly hideous, but what they lacked in talent they made up for in enthusiasm." Eddie Chamblee, who met and worked with the Beatles in the late fifties, said, "They were very rough amateurs. They knew it, had to admit it. They did give other guys credit for things they took; it helped to push them on. It took them three or four years to learn how to play. When I met them, maybe one or two were musicians. The others were just carried."

Many, including those in the rock business, asked, "How can four mop-heads attired in neo-Edwardian clothes, with Liverpudlian accents, stomping and singing a musical idiom that is distinctly American, make it here?" Why would American youths wax apoplectic over these Britishers? The question revealed as much as the enigmatic response. Something was happening here, and it would unfold in ways that no one could have predicted in 1964. There were many explanations for the Beatles phenomenon, all partial truths, as if blind men were once again asked to touch and explain an

elephant. The Beatles were at once a symbol for adolescent
revolt against parental authority; the search for peer-group
status; sexuality—both in the way they performed and in
their appeal to "material instincts"; success achieved by un-
derdogs; success by youths in a world of adults; an urgent
desire to have a "good time" in a world plagued with mortal
danger. In that year of 1964, however, no one viewed them
as carriers of a revolution. How could they? These wise-
cracking fellows seemed innocent enough. Why should anyone think of them as something other than a teenage craze?

David Riesman, asked to comment about Beatlemania for
U.S. News and World Report (February 24, 1964), agreed
that this phenomenon was a fad. "The way to describe a
craze or fad is to point out that it starts out as a minority
movement. It is self-fulfilling, self-nourishing for the minority that supports it, and every member of the minority is sup-
posed to respond in the same way. As soon as the majority
takes it up, it can no longer be a fad. Some new fad has to
come along for a new minority." What Riesman didn't note
were the signs of change that accompanied the Beatles' arrival on these shores, changes that reflected, as much as the
Beatles' reception, an upheaval in values.

A Wisconsin preacher, the Reverend David Noebel, described the Beatles as "anti-Christ. They are preparing our
teenagers for riot and ultimate revolution against our Christian republic" (*Newsweek,* February 15, 1965). In the summer of 1964, Rudi Gernreich had introduced the topless
bathing suit. An aspiring actress, Toni Lee Shelley, slipped
into Lake Michigan in this outfit (unfit?) and was arrested by
the Chicago police. When asked for an explanation, she said
deadpan, "I didn't think they could pin anything on me"
(*Newsweek,* July 6, 1964). In 1964 the fashion designer Robert Sloan introduced the "go-go-look," a split skirt that ap-

pealed to male fantasies and made it quite clear that designers had now hopped aboard the swingers' express. Graham B. Blaine, Jr., a Harvard psychiatrist, announced the arrival of a sexual revolution based on the pill. Here was a post-Kinsey report indicating that many more students now engaged in "casual" sexual intercourse than ever before. Three years later, the Rolling Stones sang "Let's Spend the Night Together" and Mitch Ryder and the Detroit Wheels recorded "Sock It to Me Baby."

This was also a time for hair. The Beatles refined the Teddy Boy look of the late fifties, but by 1964 the preoccupation with locks was nationwide. It may have been related to a Samson-like belief in virility; but whatever the reason, everyone was hung up on hair. In 1964 teenage girls spent $300 million on grooming products, most of it for shampoo, rollers, conditioners, hairpins, rinses, bleaches, lotions, sprays, and dryers. The look of that year was early Barbra Streisand, straight and natural, with the bouffant in disrepute. If you happened to have been born with curly hair, you worked endlessly to correct nature's trick on you.

Shadows of My Mind
New York Times Magazine, September 6, 1964

One of the most bizarre results of the long hair cult is that children in the 5 to 8 age group are clamoring to look like pop stars. According to Mr. John of Knightsbridge, who specializes in the carriage trade, this applies to the younger offspring of the aristocracy. He has invented what he calls a "tidied-up Stones" style which consists of a long, soft fringe and a curled-up back. His alternative title is the "uncut" look. Another top cutter, Vidal Sassoon, has created a shoulder-length bob for boys as well as girls.

Nineteen sixty-four was the year in which the press discovered the phenomenon of teenage drinking. "Drinking is contagious," said a fifteen-year-old boy. "Everybody else seems to be doing it and you get caught up in the spirit of it" (*New York Times,* July 19, 1964). Here was the consequence of easy living in the affluent suburbs. With liquor readily available, parents drinking to excess, "boredom" an excuse for everything, and youngsters seeking artificial courage to get them over the barrier of normative values into the land of forbidden fruits, it was easy to arrive at the conclusion that alcohol had answers. Four years later, Jefferson Airplane urged a generation to "feed your mind."

By 1964, Herbert Marcuse was writing and speaking about "polymorphous perversity," a way of revolutionizing society through an assault on middle-class values by the children of the middle class—the "new revolutionaries," he called them. Sex, drugs, bizarre appearance and behavior were their weapons. So, too, was the symbol of middle-class affluence: the automobile. That vehicle could provide a "walk on the wild side," a way to balance briefly on the precipice of death as James Dean did in *Rebel Without a Cause.* In 1964 Jan and Dean sang "Dead Man's Curve," an ode to the hot rod that captured the spirit of defiance and death.

> The last thing I remember, doc,
> I started to swerve.
> You won't come back from
> Dead Man's Curve.

Ironically, Jan Berry suffered brain damage and was hospitalized for several years after being in an auto crash (1966) in which three people were killed.

Nineteen hundred sixty-four was the year of Mods and Rockers, two conflicting styles that illustrated a great deal about the rock revolution. Rockers were formerly Teddy Boys, who worshipped at the throne of Marlon, Elvis, James Dean. They wore black boots and leather jackets, drove powerful motorcycles, and scorned Mods. For them, rock music ended in 1959, with Little Richard and Gene Vincent at their musical zenith. They were the children of laborers, hardened by life on the streets and unwilling to make any accommodations with the middle class. Here were the British Hell's Angels, with their own code of values and clannishness. The Mods, on the other hand, were foppishly dressed, pill-popping youths who drove chrome-plated scooters as a symbol of their relative affluence and acceptance of modernity. The Mods were artisans and office workers aspiring to be part of the growing white-collar class. They were "hip" about clothes and speech. Mod style tended to pastels and velvet with collarless shirts and jackets, horizontal stripes, and thick white rubber soles. Mods wouldn't be caught dead in a black leather jacket. Mod girls wore no jewelry and no makeup except for heavily applied eye shadow and false eyelashes. Hairdos were short, and tartan pants were in. Carnaby Street was discovered, as was the British version of rapidly changing styles. What didn't change were their recently discovered musical heroes: The Who, the Rolling Stones, and the Small Faces.

At the Prince Charles theater, the Western Ballet Company performed a new ballet entitled "Mods and Rockers" (*New York Times,* December 19, 1963). After a three-day battle in Whitsun between Mods and Rockers, a *Guardian* editorial noted: "Theirs is an ailment which can only be cured when the places in which they live and the schools in which they learn are less cramped, less frustrating and less deadly to hope.''

Back in the U.S.A., Hollywood discovered adolescence with a vengeance. *Bikini Beach,* released in 1964, cost $600,000 to make and an equal sum to promote; it grossed more than $5 million. Another of the beach sagas, *Beach Party,* did as well during its opening week in Chicago as *Cleopatra* with Taylor and Burton. In the fantasy world of teenage movies, the premium was on the bikini and those parts of the human body that were barely covered. The sex was innocent enough, and juvenile delinquency of the *Blackboard Jungle* variety seemed from another world. Girls brushed their hair compulsively and worried endlessly about their complexion. Boys concerned themselves with cars and surfing. Annette Funicello, with her mountainous hairdo and bangled bathing suits, had the largest following of any movie star in 1964 other than Elizabeth Taylor. Annette was the guardian of morals. In *Beach Party* she and Frankie Avalon arrive at the beach house to neck. His goal is perfectly clear. To their surprise and her relief, they stumble across all their friends, who happen to be there too. Annette responds gleefully, ''You know it's more fun with the whole gang.'' Frankie is unconvinced, but says in what I regard as a classic Hollywood line, ''I don't trust myself alone with you.'' He does, however, deal with his frustration by romancing a nymph in the senior class. What happens is left to the viewers' imagination, albeit Annette's code of restraint remains intact. Throughout these films sex is the preoccupation without ever being explicit.

Fifteen years later with the release of *Grease,* not only is the Annette character considered something of a caricature, but girls get ''knocked up,'' worry about their periods, and discuss nothing but sex at their pajama parties. The Beatles sang "She Loves You" in 1964, but ten years later Redbone reached number four on the charts with "Come and Get Your Love," and Exile reached number five in 1978 with "Kiss You All Over." In 1979 Rod Stewart had one of the top songs of the year, "Do Ya Think I'm Sexy?" with the lyrics:

> If you want my body and you think I'm sexy,
> Come on, sugar, let me know.
> If you really need me, just reach out and
>   touch me.
> Come on, honey, tell me so.

"Beach Blanket Bingo" went from volleyball in Malibu to cameras under the blankets. But it was the seemingly innocent teen films of 1964 that suggested what was to come. After all, even Annette couldn't remain chaste with Frankie's constant urging. Once the Pandora's box of sexual excitement was opened, the consequences were inevitable.

In the adolescent culture of 1964, heroes were innocent; even the Beatles of that era were benign sex symbols. The transference of affection from boys in school to these unattainable pop stars was a function of growing up. These teens of the mid-sixties were the children of leisure and affluence. They had the time to focus on their stars and the money to buy the icons of worship (records, pinups, rings, etc.). Instead of having heroes to look up to, these teenagers, who had the power of the pocketbook, wanted self-identifying figures whose values reflect their own aspirations. The hero was no longer an idol, but an image; not someone you look up to, but someone like you.

In 1964 teenage rebellion took the form of hero worship

for the Beatles. Fans mobbed the Fab Four, tore at their clothes, went into hysteria at their mere mention. They suggested that this excitement was a challenge to adult entertainment that purported to have a higher standard of taste. They were defiantly loyal. But the curious thing about this phenomenon—what set it apart from any condition in the past—was the lack of parental resistance. If anything, the society showed no real indication that it really cared or was deeply disturbed by this teenage fascination with the Beatles. Here was rebellion without opposition. The Beatles were different from ''Be Bop'' and ''Doo Wop'' in that their ''Yeah! Yeah!'' was not greeted by the typical generational schism. The Beatles transcended this gap and enhanced a mood in which adolescence became the dominant cultural mode, not simply an awkward stage out of which one fortunately emerges as an adult. Beatlemania was not only an abdication of parental values but a desire on the part of many parents to be a part of the action, to catch a ride on the revolutionary bandwagon.

Shadows of My Mind
Life, February 21, 1964

How to Kick the Beatle Habit:
1) Move patients as far away from Beatles as possible as quickly as possible.
2) When patient comes to, do not mention the names John Lennon, Paul McCartney, George Harrison or Ringo Starr.
3) Do not mention the word Beatles (or beetles).
4) Do not mention such words as luv, fab, gear, ciggies.
5) Do not mention the word Liverpool.
6) Do not mention the word England.

7) Do not speak with an English accent.
8) Do not speak English.

Irving Kristol defined this condition as a "temporary pathology." Perhaps it was. But a somewhat more generous interpretation might consider the dissolution of traditional customs and manners with the arrival on our shores of a cultural Lenin (Lennon?). It was the beginning of a time when reason was to give way to aspiration, when sons were to think they were wiser than their fathers, and when ideas were to be rooted in the future without a glance back to the past. That parents could not or would not confront their children with the lessons of history that describe the futility of this position is an indication of how total the victory of the counter-culture actually was. But in the blush of 1964, a new age did appear to be on the horizon. The dark clouds of Kennedy's assassination were behind us, and in front was the bright light of hope. What wasn't considered were the tragedies visited upon a whole generation that believed it could extricate its age from history, step out of the human panorama of evolution, and begin a time of justice, freedom, kindness, and love, with simple slogans. D. W. Brogan, in *The Price of Revolution,* argued, "The impatience of the young is not an excuse for the abandonment of responsibility by their elders who have noticed how quickly the rosy dawn turns into a hang-over." In 1964 all the elders could see was the same rosy dawn as the young.

The Beatles' appearance on the American scene was not a critical success. Jack Gould called their performance on the "Ed Sullivan Show" a "mass placebo" (*New York Times,* February 10, 1964). His colleague Theodore Strongin called their music "unmistakably diatonic," their harmonies "hoarsely incoherent." A *Newsweek* editor wrote that "visually they are a nightmare. . . . Musically they are a near disaster." The Beatles themselves were not any softer in their self-criticism. George Harrison said, "We're rather crummy musicians," and Paul McCartney in another interview contended, "We can't sing, we can't do anything. But we're having a great laugh." *Newsweek* called them the "evangelists of fun." *Life* magazine editors described their musical style as "embellished standard rock 'n' roll with a jackhammer beat and high screams that would do a steam calliope proud." *Time* editors simply noted that they are "achingly familiar (their songs consist mainly of 'Yeh!' screamed to the accompaniment of three guitars and a thunderous drum)." In another edition, the editors called the music "high pitched, loud beyond reason and stupefyingly repetitive."

What was truly interesting about this reception of the Beatles in 1964 was the widespread miscalculation of their influence. Most analysts saw the group as "good fun," "a positive influence" who had the "sexless" appeal of teddy bears—cute and safe. After all, they only wanted to . . . "Hold Your Hand." The craze should have given someone a clue of what was in store, since there was consensus that in this land of ritualistic fads, there had never before been anything quite like Beatlemania.

Shadows of My Mind
Newsweek, February 17, 1964

"What is the secret of your success?" asked one reporter.
"New press agents," said Ringo Starr. . . .
"Are you in favor of lunacy?"

"Yes. It's healthy," said Paul McCartney. . . .
"Which one of you is really bald?"
"We're all bald," said George Harrison . . . and I'm deaf
and dumb."

Their manager was probably more attuned to what was
happening than anyone else. This twenty-nine-year-old son
of a well-to-do Liverpool family was the public-relations advance man of this rock revolution. Brian Epstein had at-
tended the London Royal Academy of Dramatic Art and was
administering the family record business when he got a re-
quest to make a Beatles record in 1961. He decided to see the
group work before making any decisions. In his view, they
were scruffy, and their music was crude, but he sensed a
strange magnetism that led eventually to his becoming their
manager. Now he set about molding an image. He bought
them clothes, advertised them everywhere, and cultivated
their unique personalities (John, the wise guy; Paul, the
pretty boy; and George, the reliable one). When E.M.I. Records officials insisted they get a new drummer, he found
Ringo Starr, who joined the group in 1962. Epstein saw
Ringo not only as a marginally adequate drummer but as the
Harpo Marx in his re-creation of the Marx brothers.

Epstein much preferred Mozart to rock; he favored silk
shirts and silk underwear. He did not move with ease through
this world of amplified music and unorthodox behavior. But
by 1963, when another of his groups, Gerry and the Pacemakers, landed three records on the top ten, Epstein's clients
had six of the top ten spots, and he was indisputably the most
influential person in rock.

He sold the Beatles to Ed Sullivan for an unprecedented
billing arrangement. He persuaded Capitol to spend $50,000

on a major publicity program. He had 5 million ''The Beatles Are Coming'' stickers plastered all over walls in every major American city. He called disc jockeys and made it appear as if each and every one would receive an exclusive interview. He even tried, unsuccessfully, to have ''The Beatles Are Coming'' cards raised at the Rose Bowl game. He sold out Carnegie Hall for a Beatles concert in the shortest time on record. There were no efforts spared, no lengths to which he wouldn't go to achieve his goals for the Beatles. He was the advance man extraordinaire, and he also was one of the few to be prescient about the Beatles' career.

In 1964 Epstein seemed like a smooth-talking promoter; in retrospect, however, he was the strategist of cultural upheaval. Epstein sensed that a change of the dimensions he was promoting takes place integrally, body and soul, or it will not take place at all. His superficial motive was money, but in the end he had unleashed something that had profound social effects.

By 1967 Epstein was dead from an overdose of Carbitrol, which he took to help him fall asleep. There were many theories for this death: Epstein was frustrated with his homosexuality; he was carrying a torch for John; a contract on his life had been organized by business enemies; and, most plausible, since he couldn't sleep he exceeded the proper dose of the powerful tranquilizer. The theories are almost irrelevant. Like Macbeth, Epstein could sleep no more, and like all insomniacs, he had frazzled nerves and uneven judgment.

The United States produced its own version of Brian Epstein in the form of a former boxer and erstwhile record-store owner, Berry Gordy. Gordy did what no one had been able to accomplish before—he fused black gospel and pop into an entirely new sound. Gordy had a successful hit with Jackie Wilson's "Reet Petite" as early as 1957, and his early techniques also achieved success with Clyde McPhatter's "A Lover's Question" and Mary Johnson's "I Love the Way You Love." But his company did not evolve into a major musical influence until seven years later, when a fledgling trio of writers, Holland-Dozier-Holland (HDH), refined its style into a distinctive musical sound that was to revolutionize the business. Their company, Motown, was now in a takeoff stage. By 1964, with Martha and the Vandellas singing "Heat Wave," the team of HDH began a three-year period in which twenty-eight of their songs reached the top twenty. Motown sound was easily identifiable: tambourines in the offbeats, four-four drum rhythms, a surprising horn or flute "fender," and above all, a smooth, polished sound that sanitized soul for white audiences. Berry believed the music must be simple and repetitive, the lyrics unimportant and undistinguished. The alchemy was pure gold. From 1964 to 1966 the Motown "hit ratio" was about 75 percent; in other words, three-quarters of those records released made the charts. They also made new stars like Smokey Robinson and the Miracles, Mary Wells, Marvin Gaye, the Four Tops, Gladys Knight and the Pips, the Temptations, the Spinners, and, of course, the Supremes.

Gordy had built a hit machine Detroit style. He seemed to have taken the assembly-line approach for constructing cars and applied it to the record industry. In 1964 alone, Marvin Gaye had "How Sweet It Is to Be Loved by You," Mary Wells had a hit with "My Guy," the Tops recorded "Baby I Need Your Loving," the Temptations sang "The Way You Do the Things You Do," and the Supremes had their first number-one hit, "Where Did Our Love Go?" (They had five number-one hits in a row and twelve altogether—an unprecedented achievement).

Shadows of My Mind
Melody Maker, October 17, 1964

Mary Wilson:
    The record ['Where Did Our Love Go?'] made all the difference in the world. Now we are doing the big things—we are stars.

In the mid-sixties Motown had no peers. It generated a contrived music that relied on one successful formula, but what a successful formula that was! Steeped in soul, Gordy gave black music ubiquitous appeal, reaching audiences of all backgrounds and ages. He was an unwitting civil rights leader who spread the gospel of a new, less raucous sound; in a sense, his achievement foreshadowed the passage of the Civil Rights Act of 1964. Motown told the world that black performers would no longer be relegated to the race circuit. Nor would blacks be confined to roles imposed on them by tradition. The world was turning, and nothing seemed to be in its accustomed place.

    Although it is difficult to cite one year as the turning point in a dynamic process, 1964 is my selection as the time when significant portions of the public broke with adjustments to memory, compromise, and traditions. The landing of the Beatles and the takeoff of Motown appear to have conspired to invite the appearance of a new dawn. What was still in doubt at this time was the cultural order that would soon follow. However, with varying degrees of speed, traditional values dissolved under the astounded eyes of most of the population. Rock was not the ruler of this condition—a point I must reiterate. It was a spectator at the storm, but it spoke and reflected the language of change. Its role was not entirely passive: it could rekindle the ashes with a spark. But it didn't make the original fire.

If music by itself were capable of destroying social foundations, jazz, which represented values and sensibilities alien to most Americans, would have played that role long before 1964. Yet the whirlwind of emotion let loose by the Beatles' arrival and the spread of Motown reflected a cultural explosion that had a recurring social impact.

In 1964 conditions conspired to create an ambience for change. There was the emergence into adolescence of the first wave of baby boomers. A "youth culture" was manufactured with its own "needs" and pandered to with overheated political rhetoric. There were the emotional peaks of Kennedy's election and the low of his assassination. There were students everywhere; *more people went to schools, colleges, and universities in the sixties than in any other decade in American history.* There was fat-dripping, split-level, convertible-hopping affluence on an unprecedented scale. There was an election in 1964 in which the candidate who was elected talked of a "Great Society," the "quality of life," and a "war on poverty." And hanging over the society of 1964 were the dark and ominous clouds of a war in Vietnam, a war that had American advisors but had not yet created an uproar at home. Vietnam was to become to this revolution in sensibilities what World War I was to the Russian Revolution. It was lighter fluid put on the fire. The Germans use the proverb, "The soup is never eaten as hot as it's cooked.'' But by the end of the decade, many were force fed with boiling hot soup. And the Vietnam war seemed to be the fire on which the soup was boiling.

By the end of the decade, this nation was in the midst of a psychological reign of terror. In 1964, however, one could only sense what would happen. There was still philosophizing. After all, ''no revolution sweeps away the past nearly as completely as it proposes,'' argue the philosophers. And they are right. But they were wrong in guessing how significantly the revolution of the sixties would change our lives. In *Endgame,* Samuel Beckett has his characters say, ''Mean something! You and I, mean something! Ah! that's a good one!'' Those words are a perfect epitaph for 1964.

SEVEN

FRUCTIDOR—1965-1972

*I*n the French revolutionary calendar, Fructidor was the month of ripening. It was the time for buds to explode with life. The French maintained that the revolution was making utopia temporal. Nature itself sanctified the arrival of a new day. Humanity, it appeared, had been freed from the arbitrary authority of the past in favor of a rational perfectibility based on nature. Thomas Paine insisted that "we have it in our power to begin the world over again. . . ." This was, Paine believed, "a renovation in the natural order of things."

A generation after the French Revolution, Shelley wrote, "Heaven smiles, and faiths and empires gleam/Like wrecks of a dissolving dream." Tradition is the casualty of revolution. In 1791-1794 as in the period 1965-1972 people were excited to alter their cultural condition by being persuaded that they had been enslaved to whatever it was their would-be benefactors wished them to shed. In fact, Fructidor must inexorably give way to the mournful *ôse* endings of the winter months (Pluvôse, Ventôse). Edmund Burke wrote, "Nothing in progression can rest on its original plan.'' But in Fructidor of 1793 the French sang a new version of *La Marseillaise* which began:

> *Voici le jour òu la Nature*
> *Reprend ses droits sur l'univers*
> [Here is the day when nature is
> compatible with the rights of the universe]

In 1967 James Rado and Gerome Ragni wrote ''Aquarius/ Let the Sunshine In'' with the same message of natural order and eternal love:

> When the moon is in the seventh house,
> and Jupiter aligns with Mars,
> Then peace will guide the planets,
> and love will steer the stars.
> This is the dawning of the age of Aquarius,
> The age of Aquarius. Aquarius. Aquarius.
> Harmony and understanding, sympathy and
>   trust abounding.
> No more falsehoods or derisions,
> Golden living dreams of visions,
> Mystic crystal revelation, and the mind's true
>   liberation.
> Aquarius. Aquarius.*

John Sinclair in *Guitar Army* (1972) argued with all the hyperbole of this period that

> The duty of the revolutionary is to make the revolution. The duty of the musician is to make the music. But there is an equation that must not be missed: MUSIC IS REVOLUTION.

---

*''Aquarius'' by Rado, Ragni and MacDermot. Copyright © 1966, 1967, 1968 James Rado, Gerome Ragni, Galt MacDermot, Nat Shapiro and United Artists Music Co., Inc. All rights administered by United Artists Music Co., Inc. Used by permission.

Rock and roll music is one of the most vital revolutionary forces in the West—it blows people all the way back to their senses and makes them feel good, like they're *alive* again in the middle of this monstrous funeral parlor of Western civilization. And that's what the revolution is all about—we have to establish a situation on this planet where all people can feel good all the time. And we will not stop until that situation exists.

Shadows of My Mind
New York Times, November 2, 1969

Jonathan Eisen, rock critic:
  What holds rock together . . . is not uniformity of sound or agreed definitions or even a stable constituency. Rather it is a consciousness, an esthetic and a framework of reference—a new reality principle if you will.

If one discards the pure nonsense in Sinclair's statement— e.g., the "monstrous funeral parlor of Western civilization"—there remains his central point: rock and roll music is a reflection—a language—of cultural revolution. The strategy of the cultural revolutionary is to co-opt the media, to have the sons and daughters of government officials and corporate leaders digging the graves for their own class by "digging" high-energy rock 'n' roll. In the mid-fifties, in what might be described as the first stage of rock, musical complexity was sacrificed for the sake of a new audience. In the late sixties—during the second stage—the music had a message of political and social consciousness that was intended to separate believers from nonbelievers. The third stage, which I describe later in the book, is one of innovation, particularly the reliance on technique to determine the musical content.

Charles Reich in *The Greening of America,* noted that

"one of the most potent means of revolution during the 1970s is 'subversion' through culture." Presumably Dylan, the Rolling Stones, and the Jefferson Airplane—to use his illustrations—could radicalize vast audiences. What Reich didn't say is that the artist and composer writes and sings for the converted. He usually says what they want to hear. The fact that large audiences responded affirmatively to Reich's Consciousness III notion in the early seventies had more to do with the cultural distance they had already traveled than with the "innovative ideas" in Reich's book or, for that matter, the propositions for social change put forward in the rock music of that time. Rock of the late sixties and seventies was a language for the youth generation of that era. It spoke in terms and with the idiom of radicalism because the cultural revolution was at its zenith.

The rock revolution during this period was designed to shock rather than explain. At the extreme of the new culture was a psychological reign of terror; there were no proprieties, and no rational justification was required for action. Allen Ginsberg compared the Fugs to Jesus Christ. Richard Poirier in *Partisan Review* invoked Shakespeare and T. S. Eliot in describing the Beatles and saw a likeness between their lyrics and the writings of Borges and Beckett. Prof. Albert Goldman compared the Doors to *King Lear*. Benjamin De Mott wrote an article with the title "Rock as Salvation" (*New York Times,* August 25, 1968). And an editor at *Melody Maker* (the London-based pop paper) ran a headline proclaiming "Eric Clapton Is God" (June, 1968). Moderation was lost in the swelter of overheated adjectives and pretentious comparisons. Rock was no longer simply fun; it was now a "cultural force."

When Jerry Rubin told the young to "Do it!" he captured

the existential sentiment of this period. For many, the act of "doing it" was interpreted as an assault on the expressions of the past, a past that for them, at least, was perceived as one colossal failure. The very audacity of vandalizing a university building, for example, was a symbolic way of tearing down social taboos and severing an association with those who had gone before. Moreover, such action engendered the "committed spirit" that the architects of any such action deem necessary. For if so drastic a step is taken, something must be wrong. And if those in authority are unable to rectify the problem, "the people" should take authority into their own hands. In this climate the whole complex of institutions, traditions, and standards is the enemy. Rock became the expression of this existential discontent. This era of resisting authority began with the Rolling Stones' "I Can't Get No Satisfaction" (1965), moved to "People Got to Be Free" by the Rascals (1968) and Simon and Garfunkel's "Bridge Over Troubled Water" (1970), and reached momentary despair with "It's Too Late/I Feel the Earth Move" by Carole King in 1971, a year after the Kent State Massacre. Finally the irreverence was dramatically captured by Don McLean's "American Pie" (1972):

> Now for ten years we've been on our own, the
>   moss grows fat on a rollin' stone
> But that's not how it used to be when the jester
>   sang for the king and queen
> In a coat borrowed from James Dean and a voice that
>   came from you and me
> Oh and while the king was looking down, the jester
>   stole his thorny crown
> The courtroom was adjourned, no verdict was returned.

> And while Lenin read a book on Marx the quartet
>   practiced in the park
> And we sang dirges in the dark. The day the music died
> We were singin' . . .
> So bye-bye, Miss American Pie. . . .

Norman O. Brown characterized this attitude best in *Life against Death* (1959), where he preached that civilization and all its appurtenances of the past must be smashed or radically changed in order to liberate basic and presumably "pure" human urges. His view was that planned activities are futile—only the spontaneous, momentary impulses and feelings are genuine and, by his definition, human and worthwhile. As a philosophy, Brown's ideas encourage "instantism," a removal of the self from reasoned arguments and a reliance on instinct and desire. Like a religious millenarian, Brown was convinced that time was running out. He, like the authors of the Port Huron statement,* proclaimed, "We may be the last generation in the experiment with living." In 1965 Barry McGuire sang "Eve of Destruction" in which he asked "But you tell me over and over and over again my friend/Ah, you don't believe we're on the eve of destruction?"

Shadows of My Mind

U.S. News and World Report, May 8, 1967

Tommy is 16, brooding, heavy browed. In a kind of reverse protest, he has a close cropped haircut. He was the only one of the three who admitted to having taken the LSD trip.

---

* A statement written by Tom Hayden and Al Haber in 1962 that launched the Students for a Democratic Society as a national movement.

"You get a look at yourself," he said. "Maybe you don't like it, but man, you see it. You really see it."

Why had he done it? "Just for a kick. I wanted to."

With an apocalyptic scenario, sensations are everything, and the accumulated experience of the past becomes an absurd curiosity. The yesterdays are expunged through an impatience with tradition and the tomorrows preempted by disaster; there's nothing left but the whims of today. In 1967 the Beatles sang "Hello, Goodbye" which captured this dissatisfaction with the past and fear of the future.

> You say yes, I say no
> You say stop, I say go, go, go.
> Oh no.
> You say goodbye and I say hello. . . .

The combination of a reliance on impulse and an obsession with apocalypse unleashed the always present but usually controlled American penchant for transcendentalism and its corresponding distrust of reason. Unrepressed fantasy and passion and a dedication to the primitive and simple came to dominate cultural thought during this time. Steven Tyler of Aerosmith described his writing as the embodiment of spontaneity:

> I discard something that goes right to the point. I discard something which has to do with brainpower. I discard something that is tasteful. You see it's all a spur of the moment type thing. If it doesn't work, it's the wrong fuckin' music.

In its more specific ideological form this "new sensibility" attempted to displace scientific reasoning for the sake of the "humane and peaceful" society. This was romanticism in its purest form, free from the constraints of institutions and conventions. In addition, it offered its adherents the comforting effect of unity achieved through a common culture where idealism, or the thinking of goals rather than interests, was preeminent.

Shadows of My Mind
Steven Kelman, "These Are Three of the Alienated,"
New York Times Magazine, October 22, 1967

If I had been brought up in Nazi Germany—supposing I wasn't Jewish—I think I would have had an absolute set of values, that is to say, Naziism, to believe in. In modern American society, particularly in the upper-middle class, a very liberal group, where I'm given no religious background, where my parents always said to me "If you want to go to Sunday School, you *can.*" Or "If you want to take music lessons, you *can,*" but "It's up to *you,*" where they never did force any arbitrary system of values on me—what I find is that with so much freedom, I'm left with no value system, and in certain ways I wish I had a value system forced on me, so that I could have something to believe in.

Leslie Fiedler, the cultural critic, characterized this view most directly when he said, "Reason, although dead, holds us with an embrace that looks like a lover's embrace, but turns out to be rigor mortis. Unless we're necrophiles we'd better let go." This was the cult of experience in its most unvarnished condition, suggesting that feeling is more desirable than thinking. For the cultists of this contemporary transcendentalism the enemies are authority, because people are equal; tradition, because it is a form of enslavement; discipline, because it limits the range of experience. What is celebrated is improvisation rather than rules, commitment rather than judgment. At the height of this romantic cultural surge, education was not learning but a search to "discover the self." And rock artists were no longer performers but gurus leading their followers to new heights of exaltation. Steven Goldberg, writing in *Saturday Review* (May 30, 1970) captured this spirit:

> Bob Dylan is a mystic. His importance lies not in the perversion of his words into a politicism he ridicules as irrelevant or in the symbols that once filled the lesser social protest songs of his late adolescence. His only relevance is that, in a world which has lost faith that it is infused with godliness, he sings of a transcendent reality that makes it all make sense again.

Presumably Dylan saw what the scientists could not. In "Gates of Eden," the mystic that Dylan's countercultural devotees admired was most palpable. His enemy was empirical thought, which he slayed with his windmill of heavenly grace:

> The kingdom of experience
> In the precious winds they rot, . . .
> And the princess and the prince discuss
> What's real and what is not.
> It doesn't matter inside the Gates of Eden.

The Dylan songs of this period struggled to encompass the ineffable meaning of mystical experience. He was searching for salvation in the secular streets of his past. In "Like a Rolling Stone," Dylan referred to the man who succumbs to societal blandishments without ever considering the meaning of his existence. Here is the essence of Dylan's romantic vision and its implicit attack on the bourgeoisie.

> He's not selling any alibis
> As you stare into the vacuum of his eyes
> And say "do you want to
> Make a deal?"

Standing alone in the universe in the sight of God, there are no deals. In the "Blonde on Blonde" album, Dylan prescribed the life of mysticism and compassion as the way to achieve "the true self," presumably the highest levels of truth. This is not a political philosophy, notwithstanding the many political perversions that were inspired by his words. Dylan ridiculed codes and laws and even morality that claimed divine grace ("Tears of Rage"). His was a personal salvation that decried political solutions; in fact, the preoccupation with change at the expense of a spiritual experience he described, in "John Wesley Harding," as an expression of naive egotism. Dylan's search was not, like that of Diogenes, to find a wise man, but to find "the way" to salvation through a life suffused with compassion and God. Many of his cohorts followed the same path. Some did discover an inner peace; others wandered so far from life that they could not find their way home again. For still others—impatient for salvation and believing it to be derived from heightened experience—the answer was drugs.

Shadows of My Mind
Jane Alpert, *Growing Up Underground*

We believed that the world could be cleansed of all domination and submission, that perception itself could be purified of the division into subject and object, that power playing between nations, sexes, races, ages, between animals and humans, individuals and groups, could be brought to an end.

Although there is no direct relationship between drugs and music, it is also no coincidence that drugs played so prominent a role during this period of the revolutionary cycle. At least four of the songs on the Beatles' Sgt. Pepper album are concerned with a trip or "turning on." Whether "Lucy in the Sky with Diamonds" was actually a reference to LSD or was taken from a drawing by Lennon's son is irrelevant. Many of those listening to the album "pictured a trip" based on the hallucinogen.

> Picture yourself on a train in a station,
> With plasticine porters with looking glass ties,
> Suddenly someone is there at the turnstile,
> The girl with kaleidoscope eyes.

Richard Poirier ("Learning from the Beatles," *Partisan Review* 34:[1967]:540) claims that "Inventing the world out of the mind with drugs is more physically risky than doing it by writing songs, films or wearing costumes, but danger isn't what the songs offer for consideration, and it's in any case up to the Beatles alone to decide what they want for their minds and bodies." What Poirier ignored is the role the Beatles played as cultural revolutionaries. As he pointed out (they "infused the imagination of the living with the possibilities of other ways of living"), their words captured the spirit of the counterculture and, in turn, became the idiom of countercultural exchanges. The evolution of the Beatles from "I Wanna Hold Your Hand" to "Magical Mystery Tour" to "Revolution" to "Let It Be" to "Get Back" represents the entire revolutionary cycle they both reflected and helped to spearhead.

In a sense they were the embodiment of the "new revolutionaries" Herbert Marcuse described, notwithstanding their working-class background and his belief in an upper-middle-class social vanguard. After 1965 the Beatles experimented with drugs, Indian mysticism, and various and sundry causes. In themselves these actions could be described as the indulgences of the very wealthy. But in fact, the experiments had a transcendent quality. Because drugs—particularly those that tranquilize and are incompatible with an activist culture—are a challenge to bourgeois values, their use was considered an act of major social consequence. This is why drugs were so valued by a segment of the "sixties generation" and why the response to drug use by an older generation, even moderately potent drugs like marijuana, was so vehement. The drugs were a symbol challenging the social order.

Marcuse was a curious Marxist who abandoned the call for revolutionary ardor and sobriety and instead saw a potential for overturning the system through the "polymorphous perversity" of his new revolutionaries. This was the romantic side of the revolution that defied rationality. By arguing for "the suppression of harmful opinions"—presumably those different from his own—he identified what even Robespierre and Lenin found too audacious to suggest: a dictatorship of a self-admitted minority. Moreover, it was a minority that because of the "purity of its commitment" had discovered truth antecedently. One way to show that commitment was through drugs; another was through the embrace of the "right" kind of thought.

When the Beatles "dropped out" their music suggested that others do so as well. The hapless actor in "A Day in the Life" wants to "turn on" as a relief from the news of the day, the barrage of "media overkill." The Beatles suggested that one should turn inward for relief from social pressure. ("Within You, Without You.")

Try to realize it's all within yourself
no-one else can make you change
And to see you're really only very small,
and life flows on within you and without you.

But for the "day tripper" there was only a "one-way ticket, yeh," and no easy way to find salvation, despite the fact that the Beatles maintained "We Can Work It Out" and "With A Little Help from My Friends" you "can get by." These were the years of "do your thing," an expression of freedom from restraints and simultaneously a wish for a new world in which life can start afresh. Vernon Parrington has noted, "The breaking up of the static, the bold adventuring upon new worlds, is the fertile soil in which romance springs most luxuriantly." The Beatles were unlocking new worlds of mysticism and drug-related utopias. They were considered pioneers of the soul. Their followers were contemporary Emersonians who rejected materialism, feared technology, and sought to unite the human and the divine. The enemy was middle-class society with its values and wealth. Taking drugs and repeating mantras all day were acts of criticism, whether they were meant to be or not, alleged the romantic. And it is true that a drug culture imposes its values on job, property, marriage, family, class, status, power, and success.

Shadows of My Mind
Newsweek, June 27, 1966

New Yorker Walter H. Bowart, the newspaper publisher [of the East Village *Other*] . . . recommended "in all humility" that at least one senator "turn on," . . . the experiment might produce better legislation on mind drugs. At the same session, 23-year-old Eve Babitz, another East Villager, urged that Congress provide quiet parks as launching pads for LSD trips. Bowart concurred. The city is a bad place to take LSD, he explained, because while "a rose smells ten times as good, garbage smells ten times as bad."

Yet romantics—like the Beatles—were ultimately products of the society they deplored. The ability to "drop out" occurred only because he could "drop in." He could be immune to the "rat race" because Mom and Dad were usually there to help him out if need be. And he could decry the destructive impact of technology while playing his electronic guitar, watching a moon shot on television, buying speakers for his hi-fi set, adjusting his Moog synthesizer, and taking his camera to a rock concert where there would be enough electronic hardware to light up Kansas City for two weeks. In other words, even the revolutionary searching for "pure thought" was ambivalent about the society. On one day the Beatles could sing "Good Day Sunshine" and the next, "Happiness Is a Warm Gun."

By 1967 the war in Vietnam, which both conservatives and liberals could agree was being badly managed, had come home. A draft was imposed on a youthful population for a cause that was never properly explained and for which their lives were on the line. Youthful revolt now had a decidedly new meaning. The march on the Pentagon in 1967; the success of Eugene McCarthy in the 1968 primaries; the Columbia University riot in the spring of 1968; the Democratic National Convention at Chicago; and the tragic Kent State confrontation in 1970 all suggested that the war combined with the desire for countercultural reform had transformed protest into rebellion. Symbols were ubiquitous. There were the red flags for revolution, black flags for anarchism, Omega banners, and Vietcong flags of the enemy. Finally, there were American flags when Robert Kennedy and Martin Luther King were assassinated. In the middle of this phantasmagoria of riots and protest was rock music—it was the one symbol that seemed to cut through the class, status, and even doctrinal differences of demonstrators. Although cultural panjandrums with *Partisan Review* and *New York Review of Books* pedigree argued that rock was high culture and made a very elaborate case to support this position, this message wasn't translated for the people on the streets. Rock conformed to popular values, notwithstanding the obvious fact that some performers were more revolutionary than others. If rock was peripheral to social change in the fifties and early sixties, it was an integral part of popular reform by the late sixties. In the atmosphere of youthful tribalism, rock was the way to communicate when mere words failed.

Shadows of My Mind
Morris Dickstein, "Remembering the Sixties,"
Columbia College Today, June 1977

It was the first warm day of spring, everyone was in a dreamlike mood, and as we sat on the grass the campus looked more tranquil and serene than ever . . . for an instant the illusory idea of an open university in an open society, without hierarchy, with everyone doing his thing, seemed like a reality. It felt like Paris under the Commune, and proved equally fragile.

When the Beatles sang "Fun is the one thing that money can't buy" in "She's Leaving Home," the assault on bour-

geois values was at its apogee. In "Revolution" the call for
countercultural attitudes was refined even further:

> You say you'll change a constitution
> well, you know
> we all want to change your head.
> You tell me it's the institution,
> well, you know
> you better free your mind instead.

In August of 1969 an army of long-haired youths—almost
as large as the American military force in Vietnam—
descended on a small village in the Catskills for the quintes-
sential rock event of this period. They wore uniforms of
faded jeans, bandannas, and beads and carried placards with
such slogans as "Keep America Beautiful—Stay Stoned."
This three-day fair was advertised as a concert with twenty-
four rock groups performing, but in fact it was the largest
tribal gathering of the century, expressing in the purest form
the "new" generational views of communal living, hedonism, drug use, and rock music.

When a heavy rain struck this Woodstock community the
day before the main acts, the amphitheater was turned into a
swamp. Promoters got on the loudspeakers to warn that the
water coming out of the wells dug especially for this event
was impure. And they also admonished against buying *bad*
acid. More than 300 attendees had to be treated for bad LSD
trips. Doctors in the area called Woodstock a "disaster
area" and "a health emergency," and scores of physicians
were flown in from New York City. A young man tranquil-
ized by drugs was fatally injured when a tractor ran over him
while he slept in his sleeping bag.

Despite the inconveniences, tragedies, and filth, this was,

for many, the Aquarian age in practice—a time for love, joy, innocence, and an experiment in living. It was actually one part Aquarius, one part Babylon, and another part youthful combat against parental attitudes. What Woodstock also suggested was that rock for its celebrants was more than music. It became the embodiment of an ethic for "the turned-on, tuned-in" generation that dropped out of the rat race (read: bourgeois culture) for the life of revolution. Rock was partially a sideshow, but the music during this period reflected an unrestrained yearning for change, for liberation from middle-class norms, and for peace in Vietnam. The music was religion, a creed that vigorously denied dogma even when its own values hardened into a catechism. Rock's pleas for a new world were induced by an innocent response to bigotry, greed, assassination, and war. As one Berkeley student noted, "How can evil be rampant in the world when I do not know one single evil person?"

Janis Ian, fifteen at the time she wrote these lyrics, sang in "Younger Generation Blues":

> If you think I'm hating grownups,
> you've got me all wrong.
> They're very nice people when they stay where
>   they belong.
> But I'm the younger generation
> And your rules are giving me fixations.

What Ian and her peers were saying was that they wanted to change the rules, specifically change them so that "anything that makes us happy is worth doing." Here was the ultimate rationalization for hedonism. Abbie Hoffman wrote in *Revolution for the Hell of It*, "The key to organizing an alternative society is to organize people around what they can do and more importantly what they want to do.'' In a somewhat different context, Karl Kraus wrote, ''Today's literature is prescriptions written by patients.'' In the height of this cultural revolution, it often seemed as if rational thought had abdicated to youthful vexations. It was not uncommon for youths to wax evangelical about drugs as the catalyst for a new awareness, a vision of God. They rejected the terrible world around them only to create a terrible world of their own based on ''the acid trip,'' even mainlining the mystical experience.

It was only a question of time before the facts of life intruded on insouciant youths and made them pay heavily. They paid in pain, tragedy, disillusion, and finally the loss of innocence. Candide grew up to discover that life is unfair. There was clearly no way that what Frank Zappa called ''the only real patriotism of rock music'' could be the compass for a generation. The music now was reflective and occasionally reflexive, providing insights heretofore unconsidered. In the final analysis ''all you need is love'' is not good advice, a point revolutionaries always come to understand. In 1968 it was appropriate for Richard Goldstein (*New York Times,* November 24, 1968) to write,

> To do away with revolution in rock, one would have to ban the music itself, since revolt is inherent in its nature as a charged version of blues.

However, this was only part of the story and one segment of the revolutionary cycle. In the sixties it was enough to share something, to feel a brotherhood and perhaps have something to believe in. Mark Rudd, speaking about the turmoil at Columbia in 1968, argued that during the riots ''we felt a togetherness'' that had not existed before. Woodstock represented the same emotion, as did antiwar demonstrations where "We Shall Overcome" was sung and the names of the war dead were read as the demonstrators held hands. These were concerned citizens by and large—albeit there were many exceptions who had their own personal ambitions at stake in the "movement"—but they were caught in a revolutionary flood tide in which traditional values and institutions were submerged. Only the "movement" itself was an isolated rock that one could hold on to. Without any anchoring values, it was only a question of time before these people too would be caught in the rising waters.

Shadows of My Mind
Daniel Boorstin, "The New Barbarians," *Esquire,*
October, 1968

These people I would call the *Apathetes*. Just as the Aesthetes of some decades ago believed in "Art for Art's Sake" so the Apathetes believe in "Me for My Own Sake." They try to make a virtue of their indolence of mind (by calling it "Direct Action") and they exult in their feeling-apartness (by calling it "Power"). Thus these Apathetes are at the opposite pole from the radicals of the past.

There was another side to this rock revolution that was hard, bitter, satanic, and destructive. It was the other side of the universe from "flower power," but it was an intrinsic part of this cultural revolution. In a social atmosphere intemperate towards tradition, it was only a question of time for the next fad to arise. One could not describe an avant-garde culture during this era because at the moment of musical creation the song had already been dismissed. Styles and genres changed so fast that no one could keep up with them. Hippies were innocent and pure; the next moment they were hardened and corrupt. Students were experimental and free; by the time the next issue of *Time* came out, they had become dogmatic and violent. Unconventional ideas quickly became conventional. And freedom to be oneself ended at the precipice of venereal disease, drug addiction, divorce, suicide, despair, and violence.

At the Monterey International Pop Festival in 1967, The Who sang "My Generation" with the "nonnegotiable demand" (to use the language of that era) that either youth gains power or death is more desirable than growing old. Then they started building up the feedback into the amplifier, causing the guitar chords to become deafening. With the audience in a frenzy, guitarist Pete Townsend dropped smoke bombs and smashed his guitar to bits, while Keith Moon, the drummer, kicked his instruments to fragments. Later that same evening, Jimi Hendrix concluded his session by burning his guitar onstage. Brian Jones of the Rolling Stones—a group itself associated with violence—was quoted as saying, "I think this has gone about as far as it can go." But while he was saying that, a group in England paradoxically named the Creation was destroying whole cars on stage.

At the end of their 1969 American tour the Rolling Stones planned a free concert near San Francisco. Despite the fact that the site was changed less than one day before the show, some three hundred thousand fans converged on Altamont Speedway, forty miles southeast of San Francisco. Altamont turned into a nightmare. If Woodstock was a love-in, Altamont was a satanic teach-in. To this day it is the symbol of violence-prone rock concerts. With very few basic necessities available on such short notice Altamont became a living hell of drug casualties, fires, vomit, rowdy crowds, and finally brutal violence. Knife-wielding Hell's Angels, who contended they had been hired by the Stones and Grateful Dead as security guards, stabbed a young black man when he drew a revolver. He died later that evening, as did three others in the course of that day. Altamont didn't mark the end of flower power, but it was a graphic illustration of the revolution's unseemly side.

It was probably not coincidental that the best-selling books of 1967 were J. R. R. Tolkien's trilogy *The Lord of the Rings,* a pop Spenglerian tragedy that seemed to match the tragic despair of his readers. At the core of *The Lord of the Rings* is the story of civilization's violent decline. When one age dawns and another declines, the "little people," with their provincial narrowness, their simple love for beer and pipe smoking, rise to the occasion and come to dominate Middle Earth. This is presumably what led to the sense of recognition the books aroused in young readers of the 1960s. Ignored and underrated by their elders, hedonistic and clannish by choice, Frodo and Samwise, Pippin and Merry are chosen to lead this new society. Their moment on the stage of history has arrived, and now they must be bold and daring, they must risk their lives and give up their comfort and anonymity. This is their challenge, and it is the moral drama in *The Lord of the Rings.* Obviously many youths in that generation saw themselves as part of the same chosen band, called upon to destroy a way of life that was alleged to be self-serving and oblivious to social truths.

If *The Lord of the Rings* created a myth about a revolutionary vanguard that could save the society from itself, P. F. Sloan and Barry McGuire were Cassandras heralding the day of apocalypse. In 1965 Sloan wrote, and McGuire sang, "Eve of Destruction," which went to the top of the best-

seller charts. Their songs are studies in alienation like "This
Mornin' " in which the protagonist speaks but no one lis-
tens. With "Eve," there were many people sharing their
alienation and listening to the lyrics:

> Don't you understand what I'm try'n to say?
> Can't you feel the fear that I'm feelin' today?
> If the button is pushed there's no running away
> There'll be no one to save
> with the world in a grave.
> Take a look around you boy,
> It's bound to scare you boy,
> Ah, you don't believe we're on the Eve of De-
> struction.

The Byrds' bespectacled leader, Jim McGuinn, attempted to
answer Sloan's prophecy with his rendition of Pete Seeger's
"Turn! Turn! Turn!" (1966), which was taken from the
book of Ecclesiastes:

> A time to love, a time to hate;
> A time for peace, I swear it's not too late.©

For some it was too late. Several militant students acting
out a morality play based on their estrangement from society
and a perception of intractable government evil turned their
idealism into a bomb factory on West Eleventh Street in
Manhattan. What they didn't count on was that the destruction they would cause was not the Establishment's, but their
own. Theodore Gold, who was killed in the blast, had been a
leader of the Columbia campus riot of 1968 and then an SDS
Weatherman. Many of his friends contend that Gold had an
end-of-history vision in which everything ended in a sea of
tyranny and blood. The obsession with the end seemed to

eliminate the barrier between inner turmoil and outer violence. These children of Tolkien and P. F. Sloan had arrogated to themselves a "right" to smash things now in an effort to set them right at some later date. Bloodshed and violence were the necessary means for a bright new world. Bernadine Dohrn, several months before the bomb-factory explosion, waxed lyrical about Charles Manson, saying, "He had guts enough to send his girls to kill Sharon Tate and the other rich." It would be silly to suggest rock music in any way contributed to those fateful events in March, 1970, but rock did presage the blind rage. In his "Bringing It All Back Home" album in 1965, Dylan sang: "It's Alright Ma, I'm Only Bleeding" and "It's All Over Now, Baby Blue." In the same year the Byrds sang Dylan's "Mr. Tambourine Man" with the haunting refrain suggesting the end of idealism:

> Though I know that evenin's empire
> has returned into sand . . .
> left me blindly here to stand . . .
> I have no one to meet,
> And the ancient empty street's too dead for dreamin'.

By 1970 the antiwar groups, the black activists, and the disenchanted young had found a language in rock that created unity, even though their backgrounds and prior experience were quite dissimilar. Youthful imaginations were captured by the driving, deafening hard beat of rock, music that was for a time the anthem of revolution. The Jefferson Airplane, one of the first and best of the San Francisco groups, sang out the message of this period with startling explicitness in "Got To Revolution."

Rock was then a symphony of protest revealing the desire for a new set of values and the rejection of the past. Some observers of that time concluded this was a religion without a messiah; politics without statesmen. Janis Joplin responded by arguing, ''We don't need a leader. We have each other. All we need is to keep our heads straight and in ten years this country may be a decent place to live in.'' Jimi Hendrix warned after Woodstock: ''From here they [the young] will start to build and change things. The whole world needs a big wash, a big scrub-down.'' On September 18, 1969, Jimi Hendrix died in his sleep from a barbiturate overdose; on October 4, 1970, Janis Joplin was found in a Hollywood motel, the victim of a drug overdose. The Dionysian anarchism advocated by this generation had tragic consequences. Although Theodore Roszak compared the youthful radicals with the early Christians undermining a decaying pagan empire in order to build another in its place, the revolution of unreason actually seemed to bring the young closer to a New Barbarism than to a New Jerusalem.

By 1970 American theater had moved from the absurd to the grotesque. Jean Genet's evil was greeted as revelatory. Jean Paul Sartre maintained, ''By infecting us with his evil, Genet delivers himself from it.'' But what did he do to the rest of us? Traditional esthetics no longer seemed applicable. Plays by Beckett, poetry by Allen Ginsberg, essays by Eldridge Cleaver, and films by Fellini satirized the ugly and cruel by being more ugly and cruel than that which they satirized. It was as if images of beauty and civility had been forgotten by a culture in a state of amnesia. The critics who accepted the ''new esthetic'' wrote books with such titles as *Waiting for the End* (Leslie Fiedler) and *Beyond Alienation* (Marcus Klein). One hundred years before, in 1871, Dostoevsky had written *The Possessed,* which was based on the actual case of a revolutionary student murdered for a breach of discipline by others in his secret cell. What the book suggests, and what was illuminating in it for the 1970s, was a distaste for liberal rationalism and for standards of decency and culture. Dadaism took as its slogan "Destruction is also creation"; it was also an appropriate slogan for this era.

Shadows of My Mind
Newsweek, March 22, 1965

When *Newsweek* asked Yale students whom they most admired, the most common answer was "Nobody."

In 1966, Stephen Stills wrote "For What It's Worth," which was sung by Buffalo Springfield. The initial lines, which describe a movement whose meaning "ain't exactly clear," are the opening gambit for the late sixties and the seventies. It wasn't clear to Lennon and McCartney either, but in "Eleanor Rigby" (1966) they attempted to explain with the existential argument, "Eleanor Rigby/Died in the church and was buried along with her name./Nobody came." But the real André Breton of this time was Phil Ochs, who wrote poetic lines in "Crucifixion" remarkably reminiscent of his Dadaist forebears:

> And the night comes again to the circle-studded sky,
> The stars settle slowly, in loneliness they lie.
> Till the universe explodes as a falling star is raised;
> The planets are paralyzed, the mountains are amazed;
> But they all glow brighter from the brilliance of
>   the blaze;
> With the speed of insanity, then, he dies!

The reason why the unusual could be accepted as commonplace during this period is that change was imminent. Either intellectuals referred to Vico, "I think we're at the beginning of a new civilization," or the young quoted Bob Dylan, "The times they are a-changin'." Andrew Kopkind in the *New York Times* (November 10, 1968) wrote, "To be a revolutionary is to love your life enough to change it . . . to risk everything with only the glimmering hope of a world to win." Albert Camus, examining social change in the West, said, "It is a matter of style." And that it was. To be a member of the times one had to be a poseur—a stylist of the new cultural forms. In order to contrast themselves with the Beatles, who despite their hirsute and iconoclastic manner were considered charming and "wholesome," the Rolling Stones cultivated the image of England's bad boys. They were cast as Marat to the Beatles' Mirabeau. Keith Richards explained this condition: "When the Beatles were scruffy and dirty, we were just scruffier and dirtier. The long-haired, dirty-rebel image was pushed on us here in the States." Guitarist Brian Jones argued, "The Beatles are idols now. The kids can't really identify with them. But we, we identify with the kids" (*Newsweek,* November 29, 1965).

The Rolling Stones were originally imitative, relying on the Nashville sounds of Chuck Berry and on Muddy Waters, whose "Rolling Stone Blues" gave the group its name. Through the sixties the group evolved into a folk-rock, rhythm-and-blues meld that borrowed heavily from Dylan and Little Richard, without the former's interest in politics or the latter's spontaneity. What the young saw and exalted was a gutsy, sharp-edged old blues group and the unique wailing of a consummate performer, Mick Jagger, who in his carnival coxcomb outfit could jerk, shuffle, wiggle his rear, and elicit shrieks and cries from his admiring fans.

When asked about his shrieks, Jagger said, "It's a noise we make. That's all. You could be kind and call it music."

Wherever the Stones appeared in the sixties, they ignited havoc and hysteria. In Zurich in the summer of 1966 twelve thousand fans rioted and tore apart the seats in a local stadium. In Warsaw eight thousand teenagers crashed through the barriers and stormed the iron gates of the Palace of Culture. Police used tear gas and guard dogs to control the unruly crowds at three other European capitals during a Stones tour. Their unique appeal of scowls, surly talk, and suggestive lyrics was precisely what a rebellious portion of the young wanted to hear.

When the London papers ran headlines asking, "Would you want your daughter to marry a Rolling Stone?" their popularity increased. In the case of the Rolling Stones, perversity paid. They became the symbol of teenage revolt. Although they vigorously denied playing up the rebel image, their songs were a reflection of intractable youth and included heavy doses of sexual allusion (albeit they did alter the words to "Let's Spend the Night Together" for an appearance on the *Ed Sullivan Show*). Andrew Oldham, the Stones' manager, contended that the Stones only gave audiences what they wanted: "Pop music is sex and you have to hit them in the face with it."

Brazenly they thumbed their collective noses at respectable standards. German actress Anita Pallenberg, a girlfriend of Brian Jones, gave birth to Keith Richards's child. Actress Marianne Faithful, not yet divorced from her first husband, became pregnant by Mick Jagger. Said Jagger, "I am going to be a father, but I will not get married. I don't give a damn about convention." Bill Wyman was divorced from his wife with both sides readily admitting adultery. Brian Jones quit the group in 1969 and was later found drowned in his own swimming pool under the influence of drugs.

These facts are not recalled for their voyeuristic appeal but because they are illustrative of the unconventional life-style lived and advocated by the group and because the Stones's lives became the embodiment of their music. In 1969, with a microphone defiantly put between his legs, Jagger sang "Midnight Rambler," a bizarre and demonic rhapsody to rape:

> I'm going to smash down all your plate
> glass windows,
> Put a fist through your steel plate door.
> I'll stick my knife right down your throat.
> Baby. And it hurts.

Yet what the group was and what it was thought to be were quite different. Jagger noted: "Sometimes I wish I wasn't me. I don't mean the real me—I'm quite happy with that— but the person they all swear at. But every time someone curses me, I think: remember, remember, that's what makes me very rich."

At times, however, the Stones's posturing converged with reality, making the appearance of tragedy the actual thing. They seemed only to play with Satan's fire, but like so many others of this generation, they got burned in the encounter. When "Sticky Fingers" was released in 1971, a serpentine red tongue coiled sadistically on the jacket cover once again reminded Stones fans of the evil lurking on the record. After an eighteen-month period of introspection following Altamont, the Stones returned to the milieu that nurtured their music—violence, drugs, and self-destruction. British critic Geoffrey Cannon described this album as "aggressive and sexually brutal," "roaring white rock." The song "Can't You Hear Me Knocking" begins, "Yeah, you've got plastic boots. Y'all got cocaine eyes. Yeah, you got speed freak jive." Then there is "Sister Morphine" with the mournful chord progression and the words

> Oh can't you see I am fadin' fast
> And that this shot will be my last.

What the Stones portended was open revolt between the teeny boppers and their parents and, perhaps, the corollary concern of social entropy. The world seemed to be going to hell in a handbasket, and if you needed evidence for the claim, the Stones could easily provide it. There was hardly a convention they didn't assault. Jagger wrote about LSD in "Something Happened to Me Yesterday," attacked the institution of marriage and made ritualistic combat with puritan morality and genteel culture in "Salt of the Earth."

After a time Jagger and the others not only lived the life of art, they were sucked into the life of decadence. In a marginal album released in 1972, "Exile on Main Street," the obsession with sex as liberation was hammered at fans *ad nauseam.*

But even when their albums are not successful, the Rolling Stones know how to rouse an audience. They are the last mythic link to the counterculture of the sixties, and their recent album "Tattoo You" and the subsequent national tour suggest that they can generate an excitement that is the musical equivalent of once again being at the barricades.

Janis Joplin, a white woman, sang the blues, a black man's music, because she was born with ready-made grief. In fact, it came out of every pore. No matter how she tried, she couldn't exorcise the devils that haunted her. One song summed up her life: "Kozmic Blues."

Joplin was the consummate performer. In athletic jargon, she always gave 100 percent. She simply didn't know how to hold back. As she put it, "I'd rather not sing than sing quiet." Hers was not a music of sweet tones; it was raw, elemental power that was barbaric and sensual. It had all the passion of a tigress in heat; all her emotions were on display. "Look at me, man," she once said, "I'm selling my heart."

Her appetites were voracious. She lived her life as if each breath were her last. Sex, alcohol, cars, pills filled her days and nights until day and night were the same. "Whatever you need, get it now," she would often say. "The other way you end up old and who needs it?" Joplin did not end up old. She died at twenty-seven from an overdose of heroin, burned out, some might say, by an excess of feeling. When Joplin wrote her own obituary in the lyrics of a song on her unfinished album she was a "Woman Left Lonely."

What people remember about Joplin was a shy, belligerently vulnerable woman-child who let obscenities drip from her lips like water from a spout and who sang as if she had lived on the Mississippi delta all her life. In high school in Texas she was a recluse, a condition brought on by her strange appearance and manner. But after she left for San Francisco and made her way to the Monterey festival, her star burned with an incandescence rarely approached in rock history. She sang "Love Is a Ball and Chain," which was as sincere an admission as Joplin could make. She also said, "I love being a star more than life itself." Joplin contended, "You can fill your life up with ideas and go home alone. When I sing, I'm just feeling that love and lust and warm touching thing inside your body that everybody digs."

Intuitively Joplin sensed that self-destruction was part of

her appeal. She was a walk on the wild and grim side of the counterculture, a flirtation with death itself. She seemed to be a living caricature of the best and worst of youth culture. Her energy was inexhaustible, as was her desire for new "highs." Her voice was scarred by Southern Comfort and unfiltered cigarettes, but she knew how to reach an audience. Her songs were prophetic. She seemed to be compelled to explore her destructive habits; she was caught in an inexorable chain of events in which her own will was subordinate to fate.

The only way she felt free was singing. Her favorite metaphor was singing as sex and sex as liberation; the former was her release, the latter the first law of the cultural revolution. Yet in suggesting this, she was trapped into being both a lusty hedonist and a suffering woman. She needed the admiration of her audience and got it by being more irreverent, more outrageous at each concert than she was the time before. Ellen Willis, rock critic, described this state as "rebellious acquiescence"—a condition in which "the more she gave the less she got." It was no coincidence that Joplin coined the epitaph for this period with the lyrics from "Cheap Thrills," that refer to freedom's tenuous grip on the attitude of rebellion. Those sentiments rang through the corridors of revolution and echoed into the streets. The bitter words of liberation hinted at death's role as the final liberator from all the obligations of life. In Joplin's case her death, like her planetary flame, lit up a generation; it gave it the impulse for revolution, but it also taught that light and heat come from fire. You can't have the benefits without the intrinsic dangers.

Shadows of My Mind
Earl Shorris, "Love Is Dead," *New York Times Magazine,* October 29, 1967

Sex in the hippie world belongs to the seniors; the freshmen

just arrived from Connecticut and Minnesota find there are
five boys to every girl and the girls want the drug peddlers or
musicians or any boy who has established himself as the hippie version of the letter man. The best the freshmen can hope
for is occasional group sex in a crash pad, a homosexual experience or a gang rape. While their parents are studying the
Kama Sutra in a suburban bedroom in an effort to find the
joys they imagine their children get spontaneously, the children are having sex, if at all, in the style their parents have
forsaken as too square for the swinging sixties.

The revolutionary mythmakers of this period, the group
that pushed the Beatles fans off the precipice of musical convention, were The Who. If the rock revolution began as
youthful despair with parental authority, The Who reflected
violence and destruction. They didn't hint at violence as the
Rolling Stones did; they gave their audiences the psychological equivalent of the guillotine. The Who was the champion
of mod style; "My Generation" was its subgroup pledge to
clannishness and to death before compromise. When Peter
Townsend damaged his guitar on the low ceiling of the Rail-
way Tavern in Brighton (1964) and subsequently smashed it
into splinters, he fashioned the destructive act that was to
give this group international notoriety. By their own admission, group members didn't have the technical competence
to get by with their music alone. They relied on flamboy-
ance. Their appearance at the Monterey Pop Festival (1967)
brought The Who acclaim it had never achieved before and
gave the group an opportunity to have its albums played on
FM and some select AM stations.

By 1969 The Who's music had evolved into the anomalous
position of being avant-garde and moddish-boot-stomping

rock. For *Tommy,* a rock opera, audiences consisted of violence-prone bikers and self-conscious intellectuals who believed The Who had constructed a new art form. In truth, *Tommy* was a farce, a rock version of Kozinski's *Being There* in which everyone takes a fool so seriously, he cannot be described for what he is. Thematically, *Tommy* is a parable about a boy who grows deaf, dumb, and blind after watching his father being killed by his mother's lover. Because of his extraordinary manual dexterity, which is related to his blindness, he becomes a pinball wizard. Later, when he is miraculously cured, he becomes a pinball messiah and finally the leader of a quasi-religious state. When he insists that his followers play pinball with their mouths gagged, eyes covered, and ears plugged—in other words, with his former handicaps—they rebel and overthrow him, and his world falls into ruin. To the young who were convinced the nation's leaders were deaf, dumb, and blind and to followers of Tolkien who read that the most anonymous and strange citizen would become the leader, *Tommy* had profound symbolic meaning. In "Pinball Wizard" Peter Townsend wrote:

> He's been on my fav'rite table,
> He can beat my best,
> His disciples lead him in
> And he just does the rest.

The least likely of heroes uses his endemic disadvantages to do what no one else can. This theme not only appeals to underdog sympathies, but it had a special appeal to those radicals who, believing they were possessed with special vision—inner vision—considered themselves among the chosen rulers of a new social order. When I saw The Who perform *Tommy* at the Fillmore East, consummating the opera by destroying their instruments onstage, the act had a strange logic. Not only did it appear as if *Tommy* would undermine conventions, but for an instant the conventions themselves seemed to have no value. In shattering these expensive instruments the psychic distance between performer and observer was closed. One did what the other wished to do. It was an act of cathartic conceit, as if the world revolved around the Fillmore and this one existential act had a meaning that would inevitably expand beyond its borders. That this was illusory is undeniable, but the power of The Who came from making it less so, at least in an ambiance in which revolutionary smoke was what one had to breathe and the acts of destruction and creation were blurred by a heightened sense of emotional dislocation.

Paul Kantner of the Jefferson Airplane said, ''There's a significantly greater communication between the music itself, the people who make it, and the people who listen to it than there was in Elvis Presley's day.'' At the height of the revolutionary ethos the music had as its sole purpose the destruction of barriers—class, social, and ethnic distinctions as well as the barrier between audience and performer. San Francisco's ''acid rock'' was an exploration in drug-related fantasies that was designed to uproot assumptions about appropriate behavior. It was as if Haight-Ashbury (L. S. Disneyland) were writing music for the nation. In ''Runnin' Around This World'' Marty Balin of Airplane celebrated the ''fantastic joy of making love while under L.S.D.'' In ''White Rabbit'' the group sings of an Alice in Wonderland that is a drug cornucopia for the twelve-year-old junkie. Grace Slick explained these songs in the following way: ''It doesn't matter what the lyrics say, or who sings them. They're all the same. They say, 'Be free—free in love, free in sex.' " Balin put it a somewhat different way: "We're not entertaining, we're making love." For Airplane and many other groups during this period, rock 'n' roll was the Sermon on the Mount, a church in which music preached the new religion.

Shadows of My Mind
Phyllis Lee Levin, "The Short, Short, Short, Skirt Story," *New York Times,* March 20, 1966

Short skirts, some say, are a sign.

"It's spitting in the eye, protesting against bourgeois values and generations past, against the Establishment," says fashion photographer Irving Penn. "It's real protest. Much of the news isn't fit to print. Things are happening, and that's what the young are lifting their skirts about."

If the chopped-off skirt is a fashion of protest, as well as Fashion-of-the-Absurd . . . it is also fashion that suits an increasingly hedonistic society. "I would say we are living in a freer society and whether you call it a hedonistic revolution or a striking shift, there is an increasing appreciation of the sensual," says Bernard Barber, a professor of sociology at Barnard. "Not just the pure hedonist philosophy of eat, drink and be merry, but of anything that delights the eye and senses. People are less puritanical."

When it came to shock value, one group, the Fugs, put their message on the line. With "Wet Dream over You" and "Group Grope" (which features two simulated orgasms) the message was clear to everyone. Fug Ed Sanders said, "There are too many taboos in society, and we want to eliminate them. Being a Fug is better than being on a peace walk." Jimi Hendrix's music was equally explicit with its orgasmic grunts, tortured squeals, and lascivious moans. Jim Morri-

son of the Doors stated his philosophy very openly: "I'm interested in anything about revolt, disorder, chaos, especially
activity that has no meaning. It seems to me to be the road to
freedom." In order to achieve this state of freedom, the
Doors advocated a metaphysical and physical passion. Said
Morrison, "We hide ourselves in the music to reveal ourselves." In *The End,* an 11½-minute exegesis of the Oedi-
pus tale, Morrison portrays several roles including some behind a red mask. In "Light My Fire" the Doors sang in
unholy praise of forbidden joys. Morrison argued, we're in
"a search, an opening of doors. We're trying to break
through to a cleaner, purer realm." In 1969 Morrison was
issued six warrants for "lewd and lascivious behavior in
public." By 1971 he quit the band; six months later, on July
3, 1971, he died of a heart attack.

Gradually the emphasis on freedom emerged from the cocoon of groupthink as pure, unvarnished individualism. Dylan sang of being true to himself. And Paul Simon, in response to the claim "no man is an island," wrote:

> I am a rock, I am an island
> And a rock feels no pain;
> And an island never cries.

As the solidarity of the "new consciousness" was shat-
tered by fads, differences of opinion, and conflicting political tactics, the music reflected these concerns. The women's
movement, to cite one illustration, rebelled against the conformist and exploitive way male hippies treated females. In
1971 Helen Reddy sang this message loud and clear in "I Am
Woman." Harry Nilsson sang an elegy to the flower children in "Drivin' Along" (1971):

Look at those people standing on the petals
of a flower.
Look at those petals pumping for a little bit
of power.

The rock music that began this period united in its purpose
to undermine the existing social order splintered into ortho-
doxies that were narrowly defined and ultimately a betrayal
of the revolution. In 1972, at the end of this era, Gilbert
O'Sullivan presciently sang the number two hit on the charts,
"Alone Again (Naturally)." It spoke volumes about the new
mood.

As is the case in all social upheaval, most people cannot
tolerate sustained periods of interference with their ritual of
daily existence. It would also seem that the absolute freedom
this revolution called for was a mixed blessing. At some
point when this freedom verged on license and the limits of
endurance were being tested, there was an outcry for the status quo ante. Human beings can only go so far in quest of an
ideal vision. This psychological reign of terror was enervat-
ing, sapping all the strength from a culture that required a
moment of peace after seven years of chaos.

Thermidor—that time after Fructidor—comes as naturally
as leaves falling from a tree, as a rubber band snapping back
into place. When a revolution faces the intransigence of its
audience, it retreats into a moment of calm. The retreat, of
course, had its trail of effects, and its moments of change
have altered the course of our vision indefinitely. But the
emotional peak had subsided, and rock music entered a new
stage in its history.

EIGHT

THERMIDOR—1973-1978

*A*ll revolutions require their time of consolidation, that period when things calm down from the fever of turmoil. By 1973, Joplin and Hendrix were gone, burned out by their own zealousness; the Beatles had broken up in 1970; the Stones were in eclipse during this period; and acid rock had retreated before sentimental melodies. The ideals and hopes were not gone, but they were frozen in ritual. The war in Vietnam was winding down to an ignominious defeat, and Watergate preoccupied the nation. The time of popular uprisings was past, and introspection was the national mood.

In 1978 Christopher Lasch had his book the *Culture of Narcissism* published. Here was a remarkable symptom of the shifting mood. A rock generation that had walked to a tribal drummer of shared tastes now turned to personal fulfillment. "Do your own thing" shed the pretense of being a group value to reveal its narcissistic core: self-adulation. In part this development was not only understandable, it was consistent with other revolutionary patterns. The austerities of the noble life according to Robespierre resulted in the corruption of public taste during the French Directory. A vision

of Calvinistic virtues inevitably gives way to moral loose-
ness, scandal, and romantic peccadillos.

This, of course, is not to suggest that the social revolutionaries of the late sixties and seventies lived as Puritans. On the
contrary, free sex and license were essential concerns of the
revolution. But the rationalizations were high-minded, perhaps naively hopeful about building a utopia. The revolutionaries denounced war, greed, and avarice. They expected
a turning away from profit and personal wealth to altruism
and social goals. They were neo-Calvinists who had little pa-
tience for bourgeois values. Their music spoke about the
dream of a new society—one free of competition, immersed
in love, and compatible with the forces of nature.

Shadows of My Mind
Christopher Lasch, *The Culture of Narcissism*

> People nowadays complain of an inability to feel. They culti-
> vate more vivid experiences, seek to beat sluggish flesh to
> life, attempt to revive jaded appetites. They condemn the su-
> perego and exalt the lost life of the senses.

Yet such inspirational dreams can't be sustained. Ordinary
people want to be released from the constraints of utopian
visions. When the revolution loses its ardor, people eagerly
resort to private pleasures and personal indulgences. There
is a renewed scramble for wealth and position.

One can see this change most clearly in a shift in the polls
of student attitudes between the late sixties and the late seventies. In the earlier polls, various forms of public commitment were invariably cited as highly valuable. A decade
later, students in overwhelming numbers cited job and per-

sonal success as their goals. Those in the "movement" who were building a "new world" in the sixties could, by the late seventies, be found on Wall Street, at EST meetings, and at "swing" parties in Marin County. This did not mean that the revolution had changed nothing. The changes were deep and substantial, and some, such as sexual freedom, were probably irreversible, but the tendencies toward absolutism and the grand dreams of utopia evanesced. Social arrangements had altered significantly. While marriage remained intact as an institution, it was buffeted by high divorce rates, "women's liberation," and sexual promiscuity. Not only had the pattern of relations undergone a shift; so too had the expectations. This revolution of sensibilities may have changed minds more than habits, but it would be an error to suggest that habits remained unaltered.

There is the whole panoply of myths and rituals that indicate a change has occurred. A handshake with an old friend from the sixties is a ritual in brotherhood resembling none of the traditional greetings. A discussion of government with products of the revolutionary ethos has the ritual of knowing smiles and resignation. The mere mention of social justice awakens memories of an attempt to build a new social order by innocents lacking any appreciation of who gets and who pays or even what social justice means.

Yet the lust for the "perfect" society died out, save among a small minority for whom the revolutionary fervor never ends. An active, intolerant, chiliastic faith became a fairly inactive, personal, and ritualistic faith. This mood is almost reminiscent of Matthew Arnold's description of societies "wandering between two worlds, one dead, the other powerless to be born." Not only did the enthusiasm for revolution wane, but the center of gravity in our population shifted from seventeen and eighteen year olds to thirty year olds. It was therefore demographic considerations as much as a dampening of ardor that introduced Thermidor.

In the period 1948 to 1953 the number of newborns in this country rose by 50 percent, by far the biggest increase in births ever recorded here or, up until then, in any other country. That baby boom crested in 1953. Over the years 1964 to 1971—the height of the youth revolution—seventeen year olds made up the largest single age group in the country. Seventeen is, as literature from centuries has pointed out, the age of rebellion. Even without the Vietnam war this period would have been a time of turmoil. But from 1971 forward the shift in the center of population to a steadily older age group has also been unprecedented. And that fact married to the cycle of revolution began to produce in the mid-seventies a change in attitude from an intoxication with ideas to conventional concerns with career and income. By 1975 it appeared as if Charles Reich's Consciousness III was more a description of the past than a forecast of the future. Words like *career options, productivity, reindustrialization* began to replace *creative, fulfilling, identity* on the pages of the popular press. With this change came—as one would expect—a modification in musical preferences, even a reluctance to admit to the obvious revolutionary content in one's music.

The Stones, for example, said their song "Street Fighting Man" was not about changing the system but about "resignation, of rebellion bound to be stillborn, of making the best of a bad situation." Jagger described "Salt of the Earth," not as an oppressed worker eager for class war, but as a message of workers resigned to powerlessness.

The Dionysian mood induced by heavy rock gave way to a quieter time of harmoniously tuneful music. Albert Goldman described this musical change as a "tragicomedy" and a "New Depression." What it suggested was a desperate desire for music on a human scale, music of some sentimentality and warmth. James Taylor's soft and reflective vocal quality seemed to capture this spirit, as did Elton John's blend of rock and soul. The "Summer Breeze" album (1972) of Seals and Crofts had soft harmonies and a longing for peaceful days. This hardly suggested that all rock of the time was purely sweetness and light, but the shift could not be overlooked as symptomatic of a change in values.

By 1971 Bill Graham had closed the Fillmore East in New York and the Fillmore West in San Francisco. It was a symbolic act suggesting the end of an era. Promoter Graham spoke of a time when "all those wonderful kids came together to share a fantasy and exchange happiness." The Fillmore West was turned into a branch of Howard Johnson's and the Fillmore East into condominium apartments.

A Cappella

Bill Graham Interview, December 6, 1981

The sixties were an exciting time for me. The world of rock and roll was smaller and closer then. It existed on my block. It wasn't the universe. It was there on the rock 'n' roll block. So when I sold out the Fillmore for four nights, I affected 15,000 people. Now that's not a Rolling Stones concert, but this was sixty-seven, sixty-eight, sixty-nine. That society was making changes—changes in clothes, race, war, women, everything. The people who came to the place where I worked were in our church, our meeting place, and while they were there they expressed themselves in a special way mentally and spiritually. We were involved in a common cause.

By 1974 Bo Donaldson and the Heywoods recorded ''Billy, Don't Be a Hero,'' which marked the end of the war in Vietnam and suggested a generational cynicism about heroism that was to some extent unaffected by the Thermidorean reaction.

Writing in *Saturday Review,* John Neary made the point, ''There are no national heroes'' (''Where Have All Our Heroes Gone?'' May 15, 1976). In 1977 Elvis Presley was dead at the age of forty-two, a victim of drugs and self-indulgence. The father of rock, this working-class hero ended his days singing indifferently to Las Vegas audiences. At the end he was a metaphor for the rock revolution. From the eruptive talent of the fifties who worked and reworked his songs in order to craft them into hits, to the stuporous, obese shell of himself that he became during the seventies, Presley had completed the circle of revolution.

Shadows of My Mind
John Rockwell, *New York Times,* August 17, 1977

Elvis will remain the founder of rock and roll in most people's minds, and every rock singer owes something to him in matters of inflection and visual style. The Beatles and Bob Dylan brought the music closer to art as it has been traditionally defined. But Elvis was and remained a working-class hero, a man who arose from obscurity and transformed American popular art in answer to his own needs—and who may possibly have been destroyed by the isolation that being an American celebrity sometimes entails. He was as much a metaphor as a maker of music, and one of telling power and poignancy.

By the mid-seventies it was not uncommon to see and hear the repeat, the replay of the past, that trip down memory lane which relies on nostalgia and demonstrates more clearly than anything else cultural exhaustion. Robert Brustein called it ''retread culture.'' In television programming it was the remake of a successful film into a series, e.g., ''M*A*S*H'' In literature and film it was the updating of Ibsen's *An Enemy of the People* into Peter Benchley's book *Jaws* and then the Spielberg film. In rock music it was taking traditional music of both the pop and classical variety—everything from ''Ain't She Sweet?'' and ''Beethoven's Fifth'' and putting it behind a combined Latin and rock beat called disco.

Instead of looking forward, one looked back—not all the way back, but to that time when the revolution began. Here was parasitic art living off the accomplishments and dreams of an earlier time as if to say, We are tired of the innovative and novel and wish to be comfortable with the familiar. It was a statement of paralysis and relief—a tranquilizer from the turmoil of the recent past and a resistance to the new.

Ellen Sander, writing in *Saturday Review,* argued ''Rock has become an establishment, a victim of the same malaise as is the Establishment it philosophically opposes.'' But how could it be anything else? Rock reflected the evolutionary tide. Its musical composition paralleled the direction of the culture generally. And now the culture was obsessed with the self—Tom Wolfe described this period as the ''Me Decade'' (*New York,* August 23, 1976). Thus it was not surprising that the reigning deity of rock became Narcissus, the god of disco.

Shadows of My Mind
Andrew Kopkind, ''The Dialectic of Disco,'' *Village Voice,* February 12, 1979

> Disco has many functions, but one of the most essential may
> be as a drug: it feeds artificial energy, communal good feel-
> ings, and high times into an era of competition, isolation, and
> alienation.

In 1977 disco moved from the subcultural scene of Latin
salsa to the epicenter of the vast entertainment industry. In
1976 Johnnie Taylor had the number three record on the singles charts, ''Disco Lady''; in 1977 Donna Summer records
went to the top of the album charts. *Saturday Night Fever*
brought the disco ambience into film. This music was manufactured; it had all of the ingredients of a well-oiled machine.
The songs set to the beat were less significant than the music
that made people dance; the message of the disco experience
was showing off.

Shadows of My Mind
Rolling Stone, April 19, 1979

> That was *Saturday Night Fever*'s great cheap moral: What-
> ever daily drudgery entraps one, it's all erased on the dance
> floor.

Whether it was John Travolta in a *Saturday Night Fever*
disco contest or a secretary invited out to a club, the dance
was showmanship, and everyone was expected to be an exhi-
bitionist. Some of the dances—e.g., the Walk—were choreographed, eliminating any possibility of spontaneity. But
whether the dance was choreographed or not, the music was
most definitely contrived, as was the atmosphere with its

strobe lights and darkened set. This was the background for a scripted version of Bacchanalia in which the revolution of sensibilities was wedded to the commercial marketplace. This was high-energy music relying on sexual titillation put into the crucible of money-making concerns.

Disco was not a music of rebellion. It was a derivative sound without a message. It was all beat. It was the music of shifting values. If Dylan and the Beatles wrote the songs for a society in turmoil, disco represented a musical respite. Daniel Yankelovich wrote in 1974 that "the students of today are predisposed to reconcile themselves to society, feel less alienation and hope they will be able to function constructively within it." Disco symbolized this reconciliation.

By 1975 "robot dancing" was a popular musical craze. Couples—wide-eyed and expressionless—glided across the dance floor, moving in precision and stopping in place like robots suddenly switched off. The rock group Devo wore goggles and jump suits as they jerked and twitched "robotically" onstage playing their paean to "de-evolution." Shields and Yarnell did a robot sitcom for their television show parodying the dance done on the disco floor.

Here was fantasy at work combining a memory of Woody Allen in *Sleeper* and Buck Rogers of the synthetic science-fiction movie. The veneer of bright, hypnotic rhythms had all the feeling of a factory assembly line. Disco relied on spectacle; yet the spectacle itself was automatic like the robot it mimicked. In "Disco Inferno," the Trammps used the metaphor of machines instead of the convention of love. The disco ideal was self-admiration and surrender to narcissistic urgings. Everybody posed in the spotlight, but the show was an illusion maintained by a disc jockey who programmed the evening's music in order to bring you new highs. Rita

Coolidge called it "higher and higher." The disco scene was indeed like the robot that appears free of constraint but has been instructed to perform certain activities.

It was not coincidental, I believe, that *Star Wars,* the film of the decade, should introduce a vague cosmic power called "the force" that, as Obi-wan Kenobi said, "is an aura that at once controls and obeys." This was an artful way of introducing robotlike power that is controlled and obedient. It was the message to a generation in search of orthodoxy, whose cultural roots had suffered the upheaval of revolution. Jim Jones and Charles Manson programmed their pitiful followers to be obedient, to follow a path of ecstasy behind their anointed leader. With such a mind set one must erase the past and be open to the guidance of the master.

Even the horror films of this era, like *Halloween* (1978), portray a fiend wearing a mask and moving mechanically, punishing nubile teenaged girls for their promiscuity. In *Carrie* (1976) the heroine, with robotic prowess probably induced by the Devil, shatters all those who approach her.

Our current colloquialisms indicate an obsession with machines and controls. We influence with our "input"; if we work well, we "function." If someone understands what goes on around him, his "head is screwed on straight." What these words express is the renunciation of change and the freedom that is its catalyst. In Thermidor one wants one's ego on display, but at the same time wants someone else to take responsibility for one's actions. R2-D2 may be the hero for a time that insists on loyalty as the prerequisite for boundless joy.

Punk rock, which found an audience in the late seventies, is superficially a music of rebellion, with its safety pins pushed through ear lobes. But after discounting the pseudoshock and self-indulgence, one sees the music as mindless robot rock. For example, in "Teenage Lobotomy" the Ramones sing:

> Guess I'll have to break the news,
> That I got no mind to lose.
> All the girls are in love with me,
> I'm a teenage lobotomy.

The Talking Heads, a group intentionally looking like the embodiment of the good boys next door, act and sing as if they are programmed by computer cards. The B-52's, the Cars, and the Police have adopted as their band names symbols of the presumptive establishment "enemy."

The most vivid national symbol of 1977 was Richard Dreyfuss's action in the last scene of *Close Encounters of the Third Kind:* he joins the march aboard the mothership from another galaxy, heading for a Darwinian leap in evolution—or so it is suggested. What is not suggested is that these creatures from outer space may be the metaphorical equivalent of the man-on-the-white-horse who stems the tide of revolution through control and stability.

Mass culture of this period was a great escape, both literally and figuratively. Richard Hell, a punk rock singer, won acclaim with a song entitled "We're the Blank Generation" (1977). The slogan of Sid Vicious of the Sex Pistols was "Boredom," a word worn with pride on his T-shirt.

Shadows of My Mind
Newsweek, June 20, 1977

Last year a teenager named Sid Vicious . . . came home and discovered that a pair of his pants had been ripped to shreds. He was inspired to close the tears with safety pins—200 in all—and thus was a symbol born.

In 1975 *Jaws* hit the shoreline with the provocative theme
that evil struck randomly and that all the rational intentions
of the community didn't mean a whit in the face of this monstrous eating machine. Here was Thermidor with a vengeance. The hubris of complete power to change the course
of history surrendered to the belief that there was nothing the
average person could do about the evil of society. Clearly
there was nothing new about the evil. What was new was the
response to it. The freedom much admired by the revolutionaries threatened to lapse into anomie.

The great mistake of the rock revolution was believing tradition to be merely the detritus of the next historical stage.
With tradition relegated to the trash heap, novelty became
the goal, until there was nothing novel left to do. At this point
the goals of musicians so conflicted with the means at their
disposal that they ceased to be musical. Franz Kafka made
the point that Gregor Samsa, one of his characters, is an in-
sect partly because he cannot negotiate the gap between the
demands of family life and those of his job. Since he is never
whole, he is not perceived as a human being at all. Since
punk rock is designed to shock, the music is subordinated to
visual images and outrageous behavior. This visual mugging
is the message, not the music, which is usually repetitive and
heavily laden with simple chord progressions.

It is, of course, important to note that punk grew out of
British class-consciousness. Its ode to anarchy is based on a
desire to abolish class and all it involves in the British setting.
Punk style is in a constant state of flux; it has no direction
except a general sense—perhaps the most general sense—of
rebelliousness. Cut adrift from meaning, punk style is simply disorientation.

It is, therefore, not coincidental that punk music should

catch on in this country during the Thermidorean reaction. What we have chosen to emphasize is not its class origins, but its emptiness, its deviance. In a sense, the power of its message is its lack of message. The music is the expression of a period when ideas themselves are the enemy. On the other hand, punk rock is interchangeable with rage which at once is startling and cathartic. Notwithstanding the jarring sounds of punk, it is symbolic of powerlessness. The reign of terror based on ideological conformity retreated into a parody of rebellion in which the posturing of alienation is all that counts.

One of the most successful television shows of this era was "Mary Hartman, Mary Hartman," a program intent on recycling all the counterculture flotsam of the late sixties. Mary has her marriage come apart on screen; finds nothing but dismal and joyless love affairs; cries for a lifesaver as she drowns in the emotional sea of consumerland. The question that Norman Lear, the producer, asked is, Can a culture survive a nervous breakdown? Of course there are no answers. Mary wants something more from life but doesn't know what it is. She pays for a strange kind of awareness—sensitivity—with neurosis. But aside from all the problems emblazoned on the cathode ray tube, what are we to make of this program? Clearly it must be a relief to know others have problems worse than ours. But the "MH^2" problems are bred by affluence and self-indulgence. They are the problems of too many options, of luxuries unrealizable fifty years ago. Mary is obsessed with "self-improvement" like any member of the human-potential generation, but she doesn't know what it is, how to get it, or whether it will make her happy. Ultimately, Mary responds to her "problems" by crawling into the cabinets under the sink. What Mary has is the crisis of affluence mixed with too much freedom. The change in sensibilities was so dramatic in her time that a new world was opened up for Mary, a world that had the promise of nirvana but could easily become a nightmare without a guide. Mary had no guide; she didn't even have a map. She was, in fact, a symbolic child of the sixties who found Thermidor a time for relentless, and ultimately boring, self-examination.

If it isn't Zen, then it's EST; if you aren't high on jogging, then you are what you eat. The new religion in America became personal idolatry, and the manifestations of it were body salons, health clubs, jogging, and nutrition. Nutritional quackery was the single biggest topic of cocktail party conversation. "I eat organic foods" and "I'm on a coke diet" (the substitution of cocaine for food one day a week) could be heard in parlors from Manhattan's East Side to Beverly Hills. This was worship of the self at the extreme. But where was the meaning of life to be found in these preoccupations? Paul McCartney self-consciously wrote "What's wrong with that [silly love songs]/I'd like to know/Cause here I go again." It was as if love itself was a casualty of narcissism. How can one love another when all one's energies are directed to self-enhancement?

In 1977 Fleetwood Mac had one of the best-selling albums of the year with "Rumours." On side one are the pulsating rhythms of songs that illustrate Thermidorean culture at its peak. "Never Going Back Again" appears to suggest someone who cannot live in the past, presumably the recent past of overheated idealism; while "Go Your Own Way" is a message of forthright solipsism.

One year later the Doobie Brothers had the album of the year with "Minute by Minute" and the single of the year with "What a Fool Believes." The lyrics to "What a Fool Believes" are somewhat vague:

> She musters a smile
> For his nostalgic tale
> Never coming near what he wanted to say.
> Only to realize
> It never really was

These lines, however, do seem to suggest that much of the past was the apocryphal story of a sentimental fool. Could it be that this was a challenge to the revolutionary ethos, a plea to either be honest about the past or let it remain a dream? Was Barbra Streisand presaging the end of an era with "The Way We Were" (1974)?

As early as 1973 Stevie Wonder captured the spirit of Thermidor with "Visions," a song that relied on a natural ending to all things.

Undoubtedly the archetypal Thermidoreans are the Bee Gees. While still in their teens they were imitating early Beatles and vowed in their first song to turn back the clock "To The Turn of The Century." By rock standards even their sixties music was conservative in the sense of being sentimental and lachrymose. In the seventies the Bee Gees became the disco sound for 1977–78 with the release of the film *Saturday Night Fever* and their sound track of the same name. The story line of the film was simply a voyeuristic look at a working-class Brooklyn subculture reliant on disco music and dance. But it was the Bee Gees music that carried the film. This was not music for rock freaks or disco fans exclusively; it was music for everyone. Not only did the Bee Gees' album outgross a very successful film; it also spawned the idea of a rock film with a sound track for all audiences. There followed immediately *The Buddy Holly Story* (1978), *I Wanna Hold Your Hand* (1978), *American Hot Wax* (1978) and *Thank God It's Friday* (1979).

In 1978 "Night Fever" and "Stayin' Alive" went to the top of the singles chart, and "Saturday Night Fever" was by far the best-selling album of the year. But the lyrics in these songs were distinctly personal. "Stayin' alive" meant getting by (read: earning a living) so that you could spend your time at the disco club, where presumably you catch "night fever"—that desire for exhibitionistic dance displays. As Robin and Maurice Gibb pointed out, "We don't use our music to reflect social changes . . . the minute you start being political in your songs, and want to change social attitudes, then you are breaking down their market value . . . and losing your audience." What the Bee Gees did capture were the prevailing sentiments of this truncated era in which the desire for social change was subordinated to the wish for ego aggrandizement, and politics were forced to the back burner by psychology.

A Cappella
Robin Gibb Interview, December 2, 1981

As song writers and producers, we have always thought fit that our music should go forward, to progress. No matter what the current trends dictated, we have always overridden them and thought that it was always time for a change because musical tastes always change. We have tried to appeal to everybody and not just a minority of groups in the marketplace, and to that end we have encompassed all age groups from six to sixty. That's very important, and I think that's chiefly the reason we have been popular for so long.

In a national survey of American college students conducted by Alexander Astin, it was noted that freshmen in 1978 were one-and-a-half times more likely to be interested in being "well-off financially" and "having administrative responsibility" than their counterparts answering the same questions in 1970—a scant eight years earlier. Surely this dramatic shift in values was not based on random selection. If anything, it appears to suggest that by 1978 the revolutionary ardor was on the wane as student attitudes returned to the *status quo ante.*

By the mid-seventies Barry Manilow was a musical cloudburst of one saccharine hit after another. His music is an anodyne for those who overdosed on acid rock and later on the heavy metal of the seventies. Manilow is the Darin of this generation. He returns love to music and marries rock to pop once again. His lyrics clearly suggest a return to an earlier day, a moment of simplicity. "Tryin' to Get the Feelin' Again" (1975), "Beautiful Music" (1976), "Looks Like We Made It" (1976) are pop-rock songs that convey innocence through schmaltzy violins and sentimental lyrics of the "Can't Smile without You" (1978) variety. Manilow does indeed write the songs that elicit tears from young girls ("I Write the Songs"), but ten years earlier those young girls responded to a different drummer whose beat was pounding and whose message was harsh. Although rock critics usually hold Manilow's music in contempt, they often fail to realize why the seventies were his take-off period, or why his form of sentimental balladeering was so popular during that decade and beyond.

A Cappella
Clive Davis Interview, November 4, 1981

I work closely with Barry at the creative level. I help him find

material. He wrote "Copacabana" but I found "Mandy."
He's a great arranger, producer, singer, and writer, but the
strength of his career is predicated on many things. Being the
unique showman he is helps. We work as partners to create a
musical continuity. He's the creative artist; I use my ears as
the creative executive. That's what it's all about. A & R
means artist and repertoire—find the artist and help choose
the songs. Here it's a hybrid. He writes, I find.

Billy Joel, who is more overtly a rock performer than
Manilow, is nonetheless very much in tune with the seventies
shift in cultural tastes. His "Just the Way You Are" caught
the mood of the country in 1978.

Even though Meat Loaf was singing of his inability to
love, "Ain't No Way I'm Ever Gonna Love You" (1977),
love was in the air, and Chris Christian sang "I'll Always Be
With You" three years later.

Frank Barselona, contemporary music agent extraordinaire, astutely made the point that, when people do not have
to concern themselves with simply earning a living, their
music focuses on rebellion; however, with recession and
possible depression, the cultural mood becomes conservative. "Rock people, during times like these, fall back on traditional themes like love." It is also fair to suggest that the
diminution of revolutionary enthusiasm dovetailed with economic stagflation, with the latter making the former a luxury
the society could not—and would not—support.

Rock musical sounds were fashioned for a new social direction. But so too were styles. It was not coincidental that
Deborah Harry of Blondie parodied the cheesecake look of
Marilyn Monroe and sang with a Monroe-like fragility the
1978 hit "Heart of Glass."

Shadows of My Mind
Richard Cromelin, "Blondie: Wild about Harry,"
Rolling Stone, April 21, 1977

"I try to reflect everybody's taste," says Deborah. "Attitude is very important. The music creates a mood for me physically, and then I have to project the emotions or intellectual hooks, so that's what I do." As a rock personality, song seller, rather than a pure vocalist, Deborah doesn't really care if they call her a sleazy sex symbol instead of a great singer—as long as they call her. "I'll take whatever they want to give me."

The clock was turning back. Even Bruce Springsteen, whom Jon Landau of the *Rolling Stone* described as "the future of rock and roll," is not sure which direction he is moving. When "Born to Run" (1975) was released, Springsteen was widely acclaimed as the next Dylan. But by the time "Darkness on the Edge of Town" (1978) hit the market, he seemed to be searching for a peaceful center where social activism is shunned and career fulfillment is found. Those who write about Springsteen invariably find that he and his work are haunted by the fifties. In fact, his work is all blues. As Dave Marsh, his biographer, put it, "His music is indivisible, a nondescript fragment and everything that he needed to say."

In what I consider his best album, "The River" (1980), Springsteen uses fantasies to cut across time—to reach into the future, to delve into the past. He is a cynic like Dylan, but his music transcends rebellion. He is in the business of restating the fundamental qualities of rock 'n' roll like a master artist who returns to the basic work of his forefathers. As a major voice of rock in the seventies and eighties, Springsteen may be a compass point for other rock artists. Admittedly, his star has not lit up the firmament of commercial success like a Manilow or Joel, who are clearly Thermidorean figures. But Springsteen music is not divorced from the cultural soil in which it was nurtured. He is undoubtedly closer to Dylan than to Billy Joel, but the music of the sixties is not his primary influence.

By 1978 the sting of radical ideas and the musical confrontation of an earlier day were on the decline. This was a time for reconciliation, particularly of cultural ideas. The verbal instruments for revolt were converted into rituals of self-examination. A tension and verve that characterized life during the psychological reign of terror became a scramble for pleasure and wealth. The rock music of the period turned another notch on the revolutionary cycle. It is only a matter of time before it comes full circle.

NINE

RESTORATION (?)— 1979-PRESENT

Oscar Wilde once noted, "I don't regret for a single moment having lived for pleasure. I did it to the full. There was no pleasure I did not experience. . . . But to have continued the same life would have been wrong because it would have been limiting. I had to pass on." The question this comment obviously elicits is, Pass on to what? After having lived for pleasure, to what does one turn? In the course of revolutionary politics once the height of utopian ideas is crossed, the plains ahead in some ways resemble the prerevolutionary landscape. This is not to suggest the simplicism that history repeats itself, but rather that in general there are historical patterns, albeit the specifics are always different.

As social theorists like Emile Durkheim have suggested, disorganization is not a permanent condition. People living in a state of anomie seek stability. That stability invariably resembles—in the main—the stability before the dislocation. Stalin and Czar Nicholas are obviously not the same, but the differences between them pale in significance to the paramount similarity: their power rested on the people's desire for stability at any cost.

It is tempting on the basis of these introductory comments to posit that restoration is with us. But that is a conjectural claim unsubstantiated by time and a body of evidence. What is clear are the signs and the direction. There is also no reason to believe that this era will be the test of empiricism like the one black swan that challenges David Hume's contention that swans are white. If rock music provides any clues, our age appears to be in the grip of a revolutionary cycle like the Soviet Union's in the 1920s or Europe's after the Congress of Vienna. The rhetoric still has the hint of turbulence, but the bite isn't there.

Tony Sherman, writing about the very successful rock band Styx in the *New York Times* (August 16, 1981) commented:

> Rock and roll was once a music of rebellion. Rockers played, and often lived, for the sheer, crazy, defiant pleasure of the moment. "Hope I die before I get old!" shouted the English band, the Who, 15 years ago (and one of them, Keith Moon, did indeed die, at 31 of a drug overdose). But the theme of the new corporate rocker might well be "Hope I get rich before I get old." Though some rebels—like the British punk rockers Clash—remain, groups like Styx have stopped trying to outrage the bourgeoisie and have become simply the creative arm of a complex industry. If rock music once had a dynamic need to flout convention, the five members of Styx have little desire to flout anything.

In 1981 Styx sang "These Are the Best of Times."

> We'll take the best,
> Forget the rest,
> And someday we'll find
> These are the best of times

Indeed they are, for these capitalists of rock who so well reflect the present youthful mood.

Nineteen eighty-one was also the year of the Rolling Stones. Not only did the Stones go on tour for the first time since 1978, but their *Tattoo You* album went to number one on the charts. Crowds in the hundreds of thousands came to hear them do their numbers and watch Jagger strut his stuff. On the face of it, this would appear to be the revitalization of the sixties—a time for confrontation. But that interpretation is seriously flawed. The Rolling Stones are a monument to the counterculture; they are all that remain of an era. Dylan will probably never tour again; the Beatles are gone, so is Joplin. The Stones are in complete possession of that anachronistic territory called "sixties music." They are a living memory of what was, a way to slide into the myth. But they are not a band of this time. Their old songs, despite a valiant effort, cannot be made new again. Their fans stumble into an orchestrated act of synthetic affirmation that has the pungent scent of staleness.

It is revealing that in 1968 the Stones recorded "Street Fighting Man," an ode to confrontational tactics, with the existential "No Expectations" on the flip side. Fourteen years later Paul McCartney and Stevie Wonder had the song of the year, "Ebony and Ivory," with the lyrics:

> Ebony and ivory live together in perfect harmony
> Side by side on my piano keyboard
> Oh Lord, why don't we?

This was a plea for a *modus vivendi;* the mood is one of mitigated tensions. The most popular songs of the time look back with nostalgia to another period. In 1981 Barry Manilow sang about the old songs and the old times. Joan Jett and

the Blackhearts' "I Love Rock 'n' Roll" went to number one
in 1982 with the words:

> And we'll be movin' on and singin' that same old song,
> Yeah, with me singin',
> I love rock 'n' roll.

Paul Davis's "65 Love Affair" entered the top five in
1982 by longing for a music that was "simple and clear." I
had the niggling concern that the year should have been 1964
before the Gulf of Tonkin Resolution and the Beatles "experimental period," but the sentiment was palpable. Let's
return to an early, innocent time with "do-wop," "pom-
poms" and "no cares." In 1980 Billy Joel's "It's Still Rock
and Roll to Me" welcomed us back to the "age of jive."

Shadows of My Mind
Timothy White, "Billy Joel Is Angry," *Rolling
Stone,* September 4, 1980

Billy Joel:
   "Critics who are looking for art in rock and roll or pop are
looking for something that doesn't or shouldn't exist there.
   "Journalists for the most part, always tend to tune into a
lyric. I've never wanted to print my lyrics on my LP's because lyrics are not poetry; they're part of songwriting,
they're coloring and they have to be heard at the same time as
the music."

In 1981 Neil Diamond borrowed the patriotic emotion of
Neil Sedaka's "Immigrant" and sang "My country 'tis of

thee/Sweet land of liberty.'' Who would have thought in 1969 that patriotism would sell in another decade?

There were other curious signs of restoration. In 1982 Elvis Costello, a ''new wave'' artist, released ''Imperial Bedroom,'' an album that appeared to be a conscious attempt to separate himself from rock entirely. He is quoted as having said ''I'd really like to hear one of my songs recorded by Frank Sinatra or Aretha Franklin.'' And that wasn't so far-fetched. Sinatra, who was anathema to sixties rock, became a model for singers like Neil Diamond, Barry Manilow, and, to a lesser extent, Billy Joel. Stephen Holden, writing in the *New York Times* (December 13, 1981), argued that ''by the end of the 70's, Frank Sinatra looked less like the last of a dying breed than like the father of a new one.'' In fact in Sinatra's ''Trilogy'' album he recorded Diamond's ''Song Sung Blue'' and Joel's ''Just the Way You Are.'' In 1981 Carly Simon made an album of torch songs from the thirties and forties, and Diana Ross recorded Frankie Lyman's ''Why Do Fools Fall in Love?'' originally released in 1956. Groups like Foreigner, REO Speedwagon, and Journey consistently hit the top of the charts during the period with sweet, sentimental—almost maudlin—melodies, what Peter Philbin of Columbia Records called ''a Madison Avenue approach to rock 'n' roll''—one that presumably doesn't veer away from the mainstream. Those groups, such as Hall and Oates, that sang upbeat songs dipped into the tradition of the late fifties to find riffs appropriate for their music. But here again, no chances were taken.

The exceptional rock critic Greil Marcus has said, ''There was brilliant music made in the 1970's but because it had no way of linking up to grand mythic dimensions, it lacked the charge much inferior music had some years earlier.'' I suspect that the words ''mythic dimensions'' refer to revolutionary ardor. The center of rock, like the center of the culture, is not rebellion. Rock has become a casualty of cultural fragmentation, and as the search for common beliefs ensues, the natural direction is imitation, a condition that explains why the youth of the eighties find their rock sounds in the fifties and sixties.

A Cappella
Murray the K Interview, September 30, 1981

You don't have what you had in the sixties. The times have changed. There isn't one radio station that controls the market anywhere. There are so many choices. Then there are no leaders in the industry; those who can direct the energy, thought and flow in order to create a frame of reference for the music. As the times changed so did the music.

Rock is, of course, not the only cultural medium that is looking to its past. Film has rediscovered the European gothic horror films of the thirties. Modern technologies have simply been united with the tradition of *Dracula, Wolf Man,* and *Frankenstein.* Films of the late seventies and eighties compete with the horrors of reality, such as the events in Jonestown, by becoming increasingly violent and ghoulish. *Dawn of the Dead, The Texas Chain Saw Massacre,* and *Poltergeist* are shockers that take seriously the dare of teenage thrill seekers who say ''gross me out.'' Today's movie creatures have no conscience; they represent pure unadulterated terror. Even Karloff's monster in the classic *Frankenstein* could be sympathetic to an infatuated young girl. However, it is only the extension of fear, its extreme, that differentiates the contemporary horror film from its ancestors. The fact is that Steven Spielberg has turned to the past for his inspiration. His modernist techniques should not be confused with his characters and story lines, which continue the tradition begun in Germany of the thirties and Hollywood of the forties.

In 1981 Lisa Birnbach's *Official Preppy Handbook* was the most widely read book among college students. This guide on how to be preppy, which might have been a bible for students of the fifties, had all the earmarks of prescriptive behavior for students who were mixed up by the competing cultural fragments of the present and longed for a simpler time in the past. Similarly, Barbara Tuchman, in a major piece in the *New York Times* entitled "The Decline of Quality," made the point that there has been a deterioration of standards in craftsmanship and the arts. She argued by implication that things had been better in the past (during the "age of privilege" instead of the present "age of the masses") and that we should resurrect some aspects of it. The *dernier cri* in fashion for the late seventies and eighties has comprised the styles of the twenties, thirties, forties, and fifties. The fashion industry marched backwards as the upswept hairstyle of the forties returned along with the foxtail scarf and the smart little hat. Even the miniskirt had a modest return of popularity by 1982. Joseph Epstein, the editor of the *American Scholar,* took *ambition* out of the closet when he suggested it was worth cultivating, along with individual will and dreams of success. George Gilder, author of *Wealth and Poverty*—sometimes described as the Republican primer of the eighties—made a concerted appeal for the return to the traditional nuclear family as the *sine qua non* of capitalist wealth. And Peter Axthelm, writing in *Newsweek* (August 6, 1979) maintained that America needs heroes, notwithstanding the cynical view that this age cannot produce them. "To deny modern heroism, it seems to me, is to admit that the odds are too long, the game no longer worth playing."

These signs are not hard evidence, not the sort of thing on which you bet your mortgage. On the other hand, they appear and reappear with a persistence that indicates something is in the air, perhaps a return to some of the conditions of the past.

In what was undoubtedly one of the most controversial and self-serving pieces of this truncated era, Sidney Zion wrote "Outlasting Rock" in the *New York Times* (June 21, 1981). (Zion subsequently opened a club specializing in forties music.) Zion's thesis is that the old tunes of Berlin, Porter, Harburg, et al. are coming back, while rock is on the wane. Not only is rock 'n' roll not here to stay, but the Sinatra, Bennett, Tormé counterrevolution is on the way. In most respects this is a fatuous argument, thinly supported, obliquely conspiratorial, and without any understanding of rock music. That it should be published in 1981, however, is revealing. Something is happening to rock. It is probably not the resurgence of big-band sounds, but it may be different from the music of the last twenty years. Zion is unwittingly sensitive to the change. What he doesn't realize is that rock is chameleonic in a way that was not true of its pop-music ancestors. Even as demographic patterns shift to reflect an older population, audiences won't demand Bennett and Rosemary Clooney, but Presley and Berry. Rock is not simply the music for a generation, like bebop; it is the national, perhaps international, language for a revolution in sensibilities. Even when reality intrudes on the illusion of change that rock has helped to foster, and people want sober responses to the frenzy and trancelike state produced by the rock of the past, rock music will be there as a new form, or maybe an old form, but still very much rock 'n' roll.

A Cappella
Ahmet Ertegun Interview, October 17, 1981

Mr. Zion's assessment of rock music is based on wishful thinking rather than fact. He has a very limited understanding of the subject he writes about. He wishes he—and everyone else—can listen to Bing Crosby. Well they can. But the important thing is, there's more music of every type being recorded today than ever before. All you have to do is go buy those records.

It is my contention that a cultural reassertion of the kind Zion cites—which presumably is a response to three decades of musical "upheaval"—will take traditional forms. But these, I should hastily note, are rock traditions, traditions consistent with this "new language" and its sensibilities. If rock of the fifties was searching for a cause and rock of the sixties was a cause, rock of the eighties is beyond a cause. It is a music that has succeeded to such a degree that it is in control of the levers of power. The problem is that the music of rebellion has reached a point where it no longer has the impetus to rebel. It is a music of marvelous form with none of its original feeling. Punk rock, which is the last vestige of rebellion, doesn't have the following necessary to sustain itself. And country and Western, which existed outside of the pop-rock sphere, has lost its idiosyncratic sound and audience as Kenny Rodgers, Eddie Rabbit, Dolly Parton, and Crystal Gale make it MOR (middle of the road). In short, co-optation is a sign of restoration.

A Cappella

Clive Davis Interview, November 4, 1981

Musical tastes change every few years. What could have been a hit ten years ago, would not be a hit today. What was a hit five years ago, might not be a hit today. A traditional love song could not be a hit today. More is required. Music that was coming out of Broadway thirty years ago—*My Fair Lady, South Pacific, Sound of Music*—are not hits today. Now songs must be deeply emotional. There has to be a tug there; they might be less sophisticated lyrics than Cole Porter or Hammerstein. But the ballad of today affects your emotions more. You can't just admire the wit and cleverness; it's got to grab you. As rock broadens itself into more soft music—like Foreigner, REO Speedwagon, and Billy Joel stuff—you find the appeal is enormous. In 1972 the biggest-selling album at Columbia was "Bridge over Troubled Water," which sold approximately 3 million copies. Well today—even as there are reports of the record business at the financial crossroads—an AC/DC album has sold 5 or 6 million, REO Speedwagon has sold that much with one album, and so have Streisand and Barry Gibb. As the music diversifies you can draw on many segments of the market.

There are, of course, notable exceptions to this theory. AC/DC sings "Highway to Hell" as a message of apocalypse and confrontation; Pink Floyd speaks of "Another Brick in the Wall" as one more chink in the armor of tradition. Yet these songs and groups, notwithstanding their success, do not appear to be the driving force in rock music. Their appeal is part and parcel of national pluralism in all areas—a fragmentation of taste. Still there are unifying themes, with sentimentality among the most notable. There has been a return to melodic music, and the message is generally benign and less concerned with offending prevailing norms.

A Cappella
Doug Morris Interview, November 23, 1981

I'm not sure there is any trend yet. This is a period of dislocation, and so far the biggest albums have not had a significant message like some in the past. The only common denominator appears to be sex.

How this will unfold is anyone's guess, albeit historical precedent is ignored at the risk of reappearance. Saint Jerome remarked that some translations of the Bible are not versions but perversions of the original. Surely this may be true with those who dip into the traditions of rock music. If the circle of revolution will close some time soon, it is worth asking— as Max Weber did in *The Protestant Ethic and the Spirit of Capitalism*—whether the last stage of cultural development is like the first: a time of "specialists without spirit, sensualists without heart. . . ." If that were to happen, I suspect rock would be reinvented in the same way people always seem to recall what gave them pleasure and contentment.

A Cappella
Frank Barcelona Interview, October 3, 1981

Music is ambivalent today, the audience is up in the air. They [the young people] are not part of the Me Generation any more, and there is a conservative trend, but it's hard to know how it will all come out.

TEN

THE FUTURE

*I*n 1807 Hegel wrote, "It is not difficult to see that our epoch is a time of birth and an era of transition. The spirit of
man has broken with the old order of things and the old way
of thinking. . . ." As true as this statement may have appeared then, seven years later Friedrich von Gentz, secretary of the Congress of Vienna, said, "We had to rebuild
what twenty years of disorder had destroyed, to reconstruct
the political edifice out of the vast rubble with which a terrible upheaval had covered the soil of Europe." Notwithstanding the somewhat extreme statement of Gentz, it was true
that reconstruction followed revolution. It is also true that
restoration was never—and probably can never—be complete.

Yet a pattern emerges clearly from the historical record. If
the history of rock is part of a cultural revolution, it is likely,
indeed probable, that this music will follow in its specific
history the general history of the culture. In this case ontog-
eny does reproduce phylogeny. However, it is not my task to
establish or reinforce a law of history which enables one to

171

predict the future, but instead to enlarge the reader's experience to forestall surprise over the "ironies of historical events." A cultural "reign of terror" was followed by a Thermidorean reaction, and as night follows day some form of restoration will follow Thermidor. The question is still, What form will it take?

John Galsworthy (1928) commented that if you don't think about the future, you cannot have one. The admonition to plan is noble, but its basis is actually quite fatuous. There will probably be a future whether we like it or not. It may not be a desirable future, it may not be a predictable future, but a future it will be nonetheless. One can make similar claims about rock music. My guess is that rock 'n' roll is here to stay—at least for the foreseeable future. Arguments about its demise are greatly exaggerated but persistent. Irving Louis Horowitz, the distinguished sociologist, asserted in 1971 "that rock is dying. It is now going through the terminal symptoms that jazz went through in the late forties and early fifties. And it will die the same way jazz did—by growing up and being transformed."

My contention is that the metaphor of death and transformation doesn't describe the flexibility of rock. In some ways rock invigorates itself through maturity; in other ways, maturity is debilitating in the sense that the pursuit of one trend can accelerate artistic exhaustion. Rock can find inspiration in regression as well as progression. It is not hamstrung by predetermination like other musical forms. Atonal music, for example, can only go so far in the direction of dissonance before there is only noise. Rock music has eclecticism as its strength. It can be a music of desire and fear. When Nietzsche condemned Wagner's *Parsifal,* he admonished that to listen to this music was like experiencing the joys of the forbidden, but that, once experienced, it opened up the infinite possibilities of decadence which threaten rational behavior. That is precisely the position of rock; it mirrors the pleasures and the threats of cultural decadence. It is the embodiment of dreams and intoxication, of utopias and hells. George Harrison once announced confidently that "the world is ready for a mystic revolution, a discovery of the God in each of us." Led Zeppelin, meanwhile, sang of Satan's arrival on earth. It is all part of rock's seamless web.

The direction of rock in the short run is clear. Rock musicians have disinterred their skeletons looking for jewels on the bony fingers. And they are there. The record industry is now obsessed with "greatest hits" and "the best of" albums. They comprise the one sure way to boost record sales. And radio stations have hopped aboard the bandwagon; they no longer play a "blast from the past" merely to punctuate the latest hits; there are radio programs that play nothing but "sounds of the sixties" or "doo wop" and stations that are entirely devoted to music from another time. For example, WCBS FM Crystal Ship is one of an increasing number of bands that make a career out of recreating the sounds of groups long gone. Sha Na Na has become a national success by resurrecting fifties rock. *Beatlemania* thrilled teenage audiences too young to have seen the Beatles on stage. This is perfect "retread rock" in which one new group pays homage and builds a career by emulating an old group.

The cultural revolution is over, and we are about to enter the equivalent of rock's Congress of Vienna. This is not a time for verbal combat on records. Certainly not all the cultural ideas of the sixties will be rejected. Sexuality has left its mark, and that is not likely to be erased. When the attractive, innocent, doe-eyed Olivia Newton-John, who in 1974 confided "I Honestly Love You," can in 1981 play the sexpot suggesting "Let's Get Physical," life is not only following art (this is a replay of Newton-John's role in *Grease*), it is undoubtedly a sign of this time and the future. An imminent Victorian revival is not in the cards.

However, it is also apparent that the music is now divorced from the emotionally charged atmosphere that gave birth to it. Rock is not now, nor will it be, an assault on traditions as was the case in the past. In fact technological advances have so changed the character of rock that technique is the message of the music. Roller disco is music written especially for roller skating. A Moog synthesizer created the bass "mood" on Donna Summer's "Love to Love You Baby" and is now *de rigueur* with young musicians everywhere. There have been several interesting experiments with computer rock that simulate and combine rock sounds and rhythms. In fact, since disco the engineer is considered as important to the creation of an album as the artist and the composer.

Then there is video rock on cable stations that show two-and-a-half or three minute film clips of bands performing. With the development of fiber optics, interactive stations, and home transponders, it will be possible to do one's own programming of visual recordings and get the music on stereo sound through a television set.

A Cappella
Susan Steinberg, executive producer, MTV,
Interview, September 29, 1981

I think the role of MTV is basically an evolution for music to use a new technology. MTV is designed to give people visually and through sound what was formerly a one-dimensional approach to music. Groups creating will be stretched; they will now have to consider a visual approach to their music. No segment will be longer than the length of a song. Because songs rotate according to popularity—as they do on radio—you have the ability to mentally tune in or tune out the visual aspect. I think if you offer people both they are going to want both.

We are finding with MTV that there are some songs that never did very well on the charts, but because they are visually provocative, they create a new life for the record.

In some sense, this is the tail wagging the dog. While new video outlets for music may mean increased opportunities for writers and for small labels, they also raise new problems. It may be fine, even desirable, to stay at home for an evening of Olivia Newton-John or Deborah Harry, but it may mean that those talented writers and singers suffering from acne will be losing a prospective audience. Chrysalis records has made a full-length video disc version of Blondie's "Eat to the Beat" album, which admittedly was orchestrated as much around Harry's visual impact as for the musical effect. Another problem with the video approach is that showing a group perform its records undermines the concert market. Who will want to see a group live after they've been seen doing their top hits from every conceivable angle in the video repertoire?

Invariably the words that appear in the vocabulary of anyone brash or naive enough to predict rock music's future are *synthesis* and *fusion*. Synthesis takes the form of bringing instruments together with electronics and computers, while fusion is the merger of musical forms, like jazz with rock or rhythm and blues with country. Ultimately no prediction can be monochromatic because any period has many forces at work, even latent counterforces. But revivalism is here and likely to remain. I'm guessing that a Little Richard sound on a Moog will be a big hit in the nineties. I'm also guessing that there will be so many refinements in rock that one will need a lexicon on each album in order to identify the musical sounds. Already there are folk-rock, punk-rock, underground-rock, and pop-rock. If two members of the Supremes were to sing with two members of Alabama, you would have country and western–Motown. The permutations are as dazzling as they are virtually endless and sometimes ludicrous. However, they do point to a musical evolution in which a variety of mergers will be produced.

Oscar Handlin contended that "to be ignorant of what occurred before you is to remain always a child." But to be rooted in the past is a symptom of pathology. To believe that "the present is the only thing that is present," as Oscar Wilde noted, suggests you know "nothing of the age" in which you live. Yet to remain fixated on a future that one cannot possibly know is silly. Presumably life and art merge in their concern for the past, present, and future. All guesses on the future are based on what we believe to be true and what we've experienced. The history of rock music began its revolutionary mode when one could claim that the past was a tyranny. But by the end of the cycle, the signs of the reemergence of the past are so apparent that one is tempted to say, "Bury me on my face; for in a little while everything will be turned upside down."

Shadows of My Mind
Mickie Most, quoted in *Melody Maker,*
November 24, 1979

It's [rock 'n' roll has] always been a circle and it'll slowly but surely go back to an R&B feel. Not in the Georgie Fame sense, but with a little more soul and reality.

In some philosophical sense that was never resolved in my reading of the classical philosophers Parmenides and Heraclitus, there is constant change and constant sameness. The world revolves, and it is the same world. Thomas Jefferson once said, "We might as well require a man to wear still the coat which fitted him when a boy as a civilized society to remain ever under the regime of their . . . ancestors." But how does one sever such ties from the past? Even a revolution has a past. Rock music, by so well exemplifying a revolutionary condition, is itself a mirror image of the cycle at work and is entrapped in a condition of its own making.

Shadows of My Mind
David Bowie, quoted in *Melody Maker,*
November 24, 1979, on his predictions of rock music
in the future

Tragedy converted into comedy
Indifference
Complete lack of taste
To be 67 by 1990
To win a revolution by ignoring everything out of existence
To own a personal copy of "Eraserhead."

Dave Marsh, writing in *Rolling Stone* (December 25, 1980) made the following poignant point about rock music:

I recently ran across a quote from John Lennon (uttered I don't know how long ago), which seems to sum up the situation. "There is nothing conceptually better than rock and roll," he said. "No group, be it the Beatles, Dylan or the Stones, has ever improved on "Whole Lotta Shakin' Goin' On" for my money. Or maybe like our parents: that's my period and I'll dig it and never leave it."

. . . While I don't believe that rock will wind up like the big bands, still playing pointlessly thirty years past their moment, I still know that right now, and probably from here on in, rock has lost its ability to grip most people in any significant way.

While Marsh and many of his *Rolling Stone* colleagues maintain that the industry itself—namely the entrepreneurs with no musical appreciation—is responsible for the decline in rock's ability to influence people, it seems to me the obvious answer to this question of influence is ignored: The times have changed. The current nostalgia is an attempt to recapture a time when rock was exciting. This doesn't suggest a failure of nerve on the part of record executives as much as it does a time when experimentation has lost its appeal. The rock of fifteen years ago that invited the unexpected reflected a social system where turbulence was viewed as a catalyst for social change. But those times—like that rock—are only faded memories or the proverbial old wine that is rebottled by contemporary musicians.

Simon Frith noted in *Sound Effects: Youth, Leisure and the Politics of Rock 'n' Roll* that "there are capitalists ready to market anything that is potentially profitable, whatever its effects on morality, law and order, or everyone else's profit." Needless to reiterate, this is borne out by my own experience. Musical imagination is not limited by record executives but by what sells. It is the government's role to provide regulation that presumably is compatible with a vision of the public interest.

Rock music has always been a way of bringing youthful fantasies together. Frith argued rock "is a leisure commodity." It is the expression of freedom for working-class youths or for students who "grind away" at degrees. He contended that rock is a source of vitality for those who must face the working day. This Marxist view is predicated on the contention that rock is an ideology of leisure designed to divert attention from the real cultural struggle and as such is a tool as much for order as for freedom. Notwithstanding Frith's assertion that capitalists will sell anything, it is his belief that "commercial exploitation" has "tamed" the music. Rock is about "not how to live outside capitalism . . . but how to live within it."

What Frith overlooks are the cultural contradictions of capitalism, those forces released in the relative freedom capitalism permits that undermine the conditions necessary for capitalism's survival. "Getting high," for example, may be tolerated in the capitalist institutions. Yet it is the freedom of capitalism that is ultimately emphasized more than its needs. As Adam Smith argued, the selfish interests of individuals will in the aggregate lead to a social good. Those selfish interests are pursued through the expression of personal freedom. That freedom translated into market choices is the *sine qua non* of capitalism.

In the late sixties, youthful freedom took the form of active rebellion, and rock was its language. It is very debatable whether that rebellion served the social good. But this was an experiment—however truncated, however much it failed—in using capitalist methods in order to live outside the boundaries of capitalism. To regard rock as no more than a tool of sublimation is to misjudge its dynamic character over the thirty years of its existence. Rock has become a different medium as our system has changed and will continue to evolve as our system undergoes change in the future.

It is already something of an anachronism to discuss "the working class" in a white-collar society reliant on services and much preoccupied with leisure. If rock is now more subdued than its sounds of ten years ago, the change did not occur because the earlier music was too threatening to the system. Rock has changed precisely because the cultural conditions of that period do not now exist and are not likely to be duplicated in the future. In a curious way the Frankfort school* that recognizes the impact of cultural forms on social control misunderstands the reflective character of rock music. The perception of this school of thought is so rooted in the Procrustean bed of ideology that it does not leave room for the possibility that rock is both a revolutionary and a restorative cultural form, that its content is related to the historical period of its conception. Friedrich Nietzsche made the point that "the enemy of truth is not lies but convictions." That, I suspect, applies with some special meaning to the claims often made about rock music.

---

*A movement of Marxist scholars concerned primarily with the social, psychological, and cultural impact of capitalism rather than its economic organization.

ELEVEN

CONCLUSIONS

In *The Picture of Dorian Gray,* Lord Henry Wotton argues that "art has no influence upon action. It annihilates the desire to act. It is superbly sterile." In some cases this statement may be undeniable, but for rock music—assuming it is an art form, albeit one for the masses—this claim does not jibe with recent history. Rock music has the power to socialize, but it is ostensibly a barometer of public sentiment. During periods of social turbulence, rock is a call for action. It is the "Shake, Rattle and Roll" for the contemporary revolutionary. But when there is a return to normalcy, rock adjusts its tempo to a Panglossian mood of "This is the best of times."

Musical tastes invariably differ with each person, but the preferences of a period reveal a great deal about the social character of the times. Rock emerged as a mass cultural form soon after World War II. It was a music rooted in rhythm and blues and grafted to a latent youthful desire for rebellion against the prevailing norms of the fifties. It was a stylistic way to create adolescent togetherness, what Herbert Read, author of *Art and Society,* called "the synthetic and self-consistent world." I can never forget the first time I saw Elvis Presley on the "Ed Sullivan Show." As soon as the program was over, I went to the only full-length mirror in the house to emulate his gyrations as I sang "Heartbreak Hotel." For days I talked about nothing but Presley with my friends. He created instant unity, a bonding based on shared admiration. I didn't think about the lyrics in Presley's songs; I was simply fascinated by his style.

By the mid-sixties the music had undergone a transition. A modern freedom (read: permissiveness) had convinced a baby-boom generation that it was separated from its "identity." It was fashionable to argue that there was a malaise of the soul brought on by technology and bureaucracy and fostered by a government and culture interested only in survival. This view combined with the anti-Vietnam war attitude inspired a music of active rebellion, a music that preached the gospel of a new social order to an audience receptive to the idea of change.

But an ideology of change cannot, indeed does not, last indefinitely. The mood of the late sixties and seventies evanesced and became, by the mid-seventies, one of relative quiescence. There was a longing for the way things were. Rock music was less utopian; it returned to the traditional theme of popular music: sentimental love.

This pattern of rock music followed the path of what I have described as a revolution in sensibilities. As is the case in other revolutions, notably political revolutions, there is a predictable cycle at work, from incipient rebellion to active forms of revolt to a social reaction. I believe the history of rock represents the same conditions. Admittedly it is fashionable to use the word *revolution.* In fact its meaning has been blurred by overuse. But I am quite conscious of its specific content and still maintain that the last thirty years represent the Second American Revolution. During this period we have undergone an assault upon and, in some instances, a change of dramatic proportions in our attitudes toward women, sex, youth, race, family, and war. These may not all be positive changes, as I have already noted, and there are areas where the attack has not been successful—e.g., the defeat of the Equal Rights Amendment. But revolution is not defined by success; if it were, the Revolution of 1848, which failed dismally, would not be so named.

For a revolution to endure, it must have affected attitudes and then social and political institutions. In some way revolutionary ideas have been pervasive. Sexual mores have changed in the direction of openness and freedom. Egalitarianism has won significant victories on the affirmative-action front. An aversion to authority has gained so much ground that most audiences accept without question the antigovernment bias in the film *E.T.* Finally, enlargement of individual liberty through judicial decisions has led to a refashioning of social order. To any foreign observer of this country over the last three decades, the evident change is startling. These are not merely reforms; they are fundamental changes in values.

Shadows of My Mind
Lance Morrow, *Time,* February 4, 1980

Americans have been steadily relinquishing their inhibitions about social consequences of their actions. . . . The social environment has grown polluted. . . . It is as if something in the American judgment snapped, and has remained so long unrepaired that no one notices it anymore.

Nonetheless, it appears that the cycle has come to an end. If the eighties have any meaning, if the music suggests any mood shift, the change is in the direction of antebellum traditions. After all, how can our children survive in a world from which the spirit, the past, and the norms have fled? Without convention and myth, there is no comfort. Theodore Adorno, discussing the music of the sixties, noted, "The subject which expresses itself expresses precisely this: I am nothing, I am filth, no matter what they do to me, it serves me right." This was said twenty years before punk rock. But I believe it is a view that cannot be sustained in our culture. Punk will fail because it isn't in tune with these times, and nihilism will fail because it has no mythology for eliciting contentment. Moreover, despite the clarion call for an anti-rationalist cult in the late sixties—a view engendered by rock music—"anti-art" is not the wave of the future. We may have bad art, sophomoric art, tasteless art, but it is not likely we will have anti-art.

The signs of cultural conservatism—what I prefer to call restorative values—are ubiquitous. But perhaps the single most striking example is the popularity of country music that intentionally relies on nostalgia, that sentimentalizes the past and upholds a way of life that people remember fondly, albeit falsely. It is facile to describe the exhaustion of modernism as if technology itself were too tired to be a part of the future. But what I maintain can be said is that the wheel of revolution has turned. We are undoubtedly not what we were, but we are looking back to determine what we will be. Steven Tipton, in *Getting Saved from the Sixties,* asked, "If we inquire into our own moral views as we have into the views of sixties youth . . . will we find traditional answers still clear and powerful?" The question, it seems to me, is more revealing than the answer. If the height of the revolution undermined norms and conventions, what except traditions is left?

Shadows of My Mind
Jerzy Kosinski, *Pinball*

All men were subject to death at any time, and, he knew, for most men their past—their lived life—was the only reality death could not take from them. Still whereas death could terminate the existence of Patrick Domostroy as a physical being, it could not terminate the existence of his music, which, being an abstract entity, would extend into the future. His music was a shadow cast before him, and as long as he was composing, Domostroy regarded himself as existing without a history, as creating the means to outlive himself.

In this land we cannot live without traditions and we cannot live contentedly with traditions. Rock as a reflection of this condition is both disruptive and tranquilizing. Its mood is the measuring stick of social norms. Restorations are never complete; neither are traditions immutable. There will be a time for renunciation and a time for approval. That can easily be seen in the short history of rock music. For a time it symbolized revolt; it is now a symbol for tranquility. Despite its brief history, rock has developed its own tradition, and during a reprieve from cultural turmoil there is a tendency to look back to that time when the music "was simple and pure."

One of the confusing aspects of analyzing rock is its paradoxical character. Greil Marcus and Robert Christgau are quite right in describing rock music as a force for youthful solidarity. But Herbert Gans is equally correct in asserting the pluralistic tendencies in this form of mass culture. The reason both arguments are accurate is that the former was based on a vision of the late sixties and early seventies and the latter was based on an examination of culture in the middle and late seventies. To analyze rock is to describe its kaleidoscopic perspective—forever changing in shape and color. It is as dynamic as the social forces that nurture it. One moment it is like the sensuous serenity of fall; the next it is bursting forth with exuberance like spring. It is admittedly mass cult, a music forever having to justify its validity. But it is also a music for all seasons.

INDEX

187

"Drivin' Along," 136–37
Drugs, as theme of rock music, 111–14, 128–29
Duncan, Cleve, 32
Durham, Eddie, 16–17
Durkheim, Emile, 159
Dylan, Bob, 8, 46, 47, 77, 78, 79, 104, 109, 110, 123, 126, 144, 147, 158, 161, 178

"Earth Angel," 31–32, 35
"Eat to the Beat," 175
"Ebony and Ivory," 161
Eclecticism of rock music, 22, 172
Eden Express, 27
"Ed Sullivan Show," 93, 127, 182
Eisen, Jonathon, 6, 36, 103
"Eleanor Rigby," 125
Elvis (Goldman), 56
E.M.I. Records, 95
Endgame (Beckett), 100
"End of the World," 78
Epstein, Brian, 95–96
Epstein, Joseph, 165
Ertegun, Ahmet, 167
Ertegun brothers, 28
Escapism, 70–71
"Eve of Destruction," 106, 121, 122
Everly Brothers, 46, 71
"Exile on Main Street," 129

Fabian, 74
Fame, Georgie, 176
"Fat Man," 65
Fellini, Federico, 124
Fiedler, Leslie, 108, 124
Fire in the Minds of Men (Billington), 9
Flamingos, 1
Fleetwood Mac, 152
Fletcher, Andrew, ix
Flower children, 136
Flower power, 199, 121
Folk City, 37
Folk concerts, 72
Folk music, 14, 75–79
Folk-rock, 176
Ford, Ernie, 19
Foreigner, 163, 168
Forrest, Jimmy, 17

Forte, Fabiano, 74
"For What It's Worth," 125
Four Tops, 97
Frankenstein, 164
Frankfort school, 180
Franklin, Aretha, 163
Freed, Alan, 5, 35
Frith, Simon, 29, 178
Fugs, 135
Funicello, Annette, 90, 91
Fusion, 175

Gale, Crystal, 167
Galsworthy, John, 172
Gans, Herbert, 185
Gardner, Paul, 81
Garfunkel, Art. *See* Simon and Garfunkel
Gasset, Ortega y, 82
"Gates of Eden," 109
Gaye, Marvin, 97
"Gee," 28, 31, 40
Genet, Jean, 124
Gentz, Friedrich von, 171
Gernreich, Rudi, 86
Gerry and the Pacemakers, 95
"Get a Job," 41–42
"Get Back," 111
Getting Saved from the Sixties (Tipaton), 184
Gilder, George, 165
Giles Goat Boy (Barth), 7
Gillette, Charlie, 6, 29, 41
Ginsberg, Allen, 104, 124
"Girl Can't Help It," 63
"Girl Named Daisy," 62–63
Go-go look, 86–87
Gold, Theodore, 122
Goldberg, Steven, 109
Goldman, Albert, 56, 104, 143
Goldner, George, 28
Goldstein, Richard, 7, 36, 118
Gone/End label, 28
"Good Day Sunshine," 114
"Good Golly Miss Molly," 63
Goodman, Benny, 5, 15, 17
"Goodnight Sweetheart Goodnight," 48
"Good Vibrations," 81
Gordy, Berry, 96–97, 98
Gospel music, 15, 20